YORK BUSINESS

GENERAL EDITOR:
Sir Kenneth Alexander

MACROECONOMICS

Gavin Kennedy

B.A., M.Sc. (STRATHCLYDE), Ph.D. (BRUNEL)
Professor of Defence Finance, Heriot-Watt University

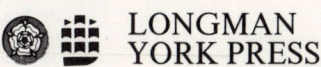

LONGMAN
YORK PRESS

For Florence

YORK PRESS
Immeuble Esseily, Place Riad Solh, Beirut.

LONGMAN GROUP UK LIMITED
Longman House,
Burnt Mill,
Harlow,
Essex.

© Librairie du Liban 1987

All rights reserved. No part of this publication may be reproduced, stored in a retrieval system, or transmitted in any form or by any means, electronic, mechanical, photocopying, recording, or otherwise, without the prior permission of the copyright owner.

First published 1987

ISBN 0 582 00346 6

Printed in Singapore

Contents

Preface *page* 5

Introduction 7

PART I

Chapter 1: The wealth of nations 11
Chapter 2: Measuring economic activity 15
Chapter 3: Circular flows of economic activity 20
Chapter 4: Government and the circular flow 24
Chapter 5: Foreign trade and the circular flow 30
Chapter 6: Components of the national income 35
Chapter 7: Value added 40
Chapter 8: The national income accounts 44
Chapter 9: GNP critically examined 51

PART II

Chapter 10: The Keynesian legacy 60
Chapter 11: How much economic activity? 62
Chapter 12: Effective demand and economic activity 67
Chapter 13: Consumption and saving 70
Chapter 14: The multiplier 76
Chapter 15: Investment, interest and expectations 81
Chapter 16: Fiscal policies 87

PART III

Chapter 17: The non-monetary economy 93
Chapter 18: The monetary economy 99
Chapter 19: As good as gold 104
Chapter 20: The creation of money by banks 107
Chapter 21: Open market operations 111
Chapter 22: The classical quantity theory of money 116
Chapter 23: The theory of natural unemployment 120

Chapter 24: Monetarist policies   128
Chapter 25: Rational expectations   133
Chapter 26: International trade   138
Chapter 27: Comparative advantage   143
Chapter 28: Foreign exchange rates   150
Chapter 29: Balance of payments   157
Chapter 30: Concluding remarks   163

Index   166

The author of this Handbook   170

Preface

THIS SHORT TEXT has been written for students new to economics. Like most textbooks it does not contain any new material but rather interprets and presents for beginning students the (hopefully) well understood existing ideas and concepts of mainstream economists.

It concerns itself exclusively with the subject of macroeconomics and follows a well trod track through the subject. The author's beliefs on how best to traverse the subject of macroeconomics might be felt by (some of) his colleagues to be a trifle eccentric at times, but it is the author's prejudice that a textbook should be written exclusively with the reader in mind.

What appears to be well understood and quite clear to those working or teaching a subject can be completely baffling to those approaching it for the first time.

I have approached my task with a class of young persons in my mind's eye, so to speak, and have assembled the materials I would use in teaching them live in a lecture room. It is the objective of the text that after reading it, you, the beginner, will be somewhat further along the road to understanding macroeconomics than you were before you started. If this is the result of your efforts then my own will have been worthwhile.

The origin of the book was in an invitation from Sir Kenneth Alexander, Principal of the University of Stirling, in Scotland, for me to write a short textbook on macroeconomics for young students. The book came to fruition following thought on how best to inform and enthuse the reader who wants (needs?) to know something about macroeconomics.

Having been taught my own first economics by Sir Kenneth Alexander in the 1960s, at the University of Strathclyde (Scotland), I decided to follow what I have always interpreted as his own teaching practice of being as clear as possible, of treating the intelligence and motivation of students with respect and of not avoiding difficulties – economics should be shown plainly and without any attempt to gloss over its shortcomings – where to do otherwise would trivialise the content.

Textbooks, inevitably, are great consumers of other people's talents. I trust my colleagues will forgive my occasional lapses in 'explaining' their work.

Textbooks are also great consumers of one's own family's time and patience. I know my own have already discounted the time I spent working on this book, but (again) they deserve special mention for being so willing, in the interests of authorship (and I hope of the readers), to put up with my divided attentions.

Edinburgh GAVIN KENNEDY
September 1986

Introduction

IF YOU EVER MEET ANYBODY who tries to tell you that economics is easy, you will know straight away that he is trying to sell you something (perhaps another textbook!) or that he does not know much about economics.

Most things that are worthwhile – and a few that are not – are often difficult to acquire, and a working knowledge of economics is no exception.

Economics can be difficult – and in parts it can also be a trifle boring – but much of it is sheer common sense, and once the initial awe at its complexity is overcome, you should be able to go on to a clear understanding of how economists think, how they see the way the world works, and why they often disagree with each other about what they think and how they see the world working!

Economists are often seen as divided and argumentative, at each other's throats when it comes to debating important issues, like the policies a government should or should not pursue in the realm of business, taxation, personal freedom, international trade and such like.

Find any two economists and you will likely find (or so it seems to outsiders) two opinions, each grounded in the same 'facts' and each as certain as the other that *his* theory or policy explains exactly what to do.

Jokes about economists abound: 'Lay all economists end to end and still you will not reach a conclusion' is probably the most famous (and with repetition the least amusing!). How many jokes does one hear about civil engineers, or sewage workers, or dentists?

Economists have suffered from a bad public image for many years, but I suspect that this is largely because the subject matter of economics is closest to the public eye – all of us are affected by the economic policies our government follows or believes in – and if the dissent and debate of chemical engineers or physicists were anywhere as close to the lives and interests of the public as those of economists, they too would, perhaps, be held in equally low esteem.

Yet economists do subscribe to a broadly similar doctrine about how an economy works or should work; what they differ on is whether a particular economy corresponds to the abstract theoretical models for which many economists are too fond of acquiring an admiration, or whether this or that policy is appropriate to achieve this or that objective (and even whether this objective, as against another, is worth striving for).

Deeply important issues cannot be resolved in this book. My purpose in mentioning them is to acknowledge what all readers will discover in due course, if they are not already familiar with it, that economics is a science with a high profile in debate and dissent, and that to study it at all exposes you to a whole world of controversies, which you must be equipped to handle if you are to make the most of your studies.

I have said that economics can be a difficult subject to grasp, particularly if you approach your studies casually and with an eye on the 'soft' option. Economics is a subject that is best tackled head on and not with a hankering after the soft option. In fact, short cuts in economics produce half-baked prejudices which are absolutely useless as guides to action, or even as guides to understanding other people's actions.

This is not to say that an author should deliberately make the initial exploration of economic ideas as difficult as possible, in a futile attempt to impress readers (and colleagues) with his own erudition. Much that is complex in economics can be understood by applying common sense to simple examples and allowing the important meanings inherent in the examples to sink into your consciousness.

Upon reflection and further study you can get to grips with the essentially complex ideas of economics and, with the skip and a jump of a newly acquired skill, leap across from the purely philosophical, or theoretical, standpoint taught in most economics courses to the highly practical matter of taking a view about the options for policy facing your own economy or those that you are observing.

In what follows I have endeavoured to bear in mind that you are a beginner in macroeconomics. I assume absolutely no previous acquaintance or study of the subject. Everything is explained, and where necessary re-explained, on the presumption that though you are willing to work at acquiring a knowledge of macroeconomics, you find it easier to work if you are guided carefully over the subject, by a sympathetic and humble teacher.

The book is divided into four parts, broadly:

Part I: the measurement of economic activity (national income accounts)
Part II: 'Keynesian' demand management
Part III: money and monetarism
Part IV: international trade

This is aimed at helping you to separate out the major themes among the thirty chapters that follow.

It is in this spirit that we approach the first chapter, on the wealth of nations. Characteristically, this chapter opens the book where the subject of economics itself began over two hundred years ago in eighteenth century Scotland. Chapters follow on the measurement of economic activity (the Gross National Product) and the components of these economic activities.

We will look at the subject of the growth of a national economy, or how it gets richer, and how it attends to the welfare of its citizens, and how it distributes what it produces. We will look at the role of central government in managing an economy and the associated controversies of government intervention versus leaving the economy alone (so-called *laissez-faire*).

I have presented the central ideas of the 'Keynesians' and the monetarists in separate chapters, and, because the debate between the two approaches (fiscal versus monetary policy) is far from over, I have provided sufficient detail to enable you to follow the debate without having my own views imposed upon you as well. Recent developments in the theory of rational expectations are also mentioned.

The concluding chapters deal with the macroeconomics of international trade: why trade can be beneficial, how foreign exchange works, and what is included in the balance of payments accounts.

Much of macroeconomics is of a technical nature but every attempt is made to make this accessible to a beginning student without recourse to mathematics and complicated formulae. Necessarily, some technical language is inevitable and you must be prepared to accept this along with the easier bits. I have deliberately kept the number of diagrams down to a minimum, believing that, if you are not in a classroom situation with a tutor available to develop the logic of each part of the diagram, they can be, in my view, very off-putting to those who come across them for the first time.

Some chapters may have to be re-read at a later date and others re-worked several times. Those who would acquire intellectual skills have to work for them! But on the whole this text is well within the capacity of the average beginning student who is prepared to persevere through the difficult bits.

As an author I believe I have written a readable introduction to macroeconomics, and I ask you in return to stick with the text right to the end and to postpone your final judgement about how difficult or interesting economics is, when, and only when, you have completed the book and thought about what it has discussed.

Economics is more than just a difficult subject to beginners: it is also an exciting science for those who become accomplished in its methods and principles. As a student, I had my own doubts about the value of the effort required to achieve a satisfactory level of accomplishment in economics; as a teacher I have no regrets whatsoever that I persevered, and I invite you, the reader, to do likewise for the next thirty chapters at least!

PART I

Chapter 1

The wealth of nations

THE FIRST BOOK ON ECONOMICS was written by a Scotsman. It took him over ten years. It was published in 1776, the year of the outbreak of the American war of independence from the British. The man who wrote it, Professor Adam Smith, distilled the ideas of many others, and added some ideas unique to himself, into one great book: *An Inquiry into the Nature and Causes of the Wealth of Nations*.

Smith's great work is still in print today, and has been translated into many languages. It is more often quoted than read in full, yet its importance as a starting point for the science of economics is often misunderstood, or worse, grossly underestimated. Consider its title: what is its real significance? Surely it is obvious that the nature and causes of the wealth of nations are worthy of study, if only to emulate those causes to ensure that our own nation is among those that are wealthy!

But the real significance of Smith's title is that, before him, nobody had thought it appropriate to spend ten years of his life developing an explanation of what made a nation wealthy. And the reason for this lapse is startling: for much of previous recorded history, nations did not become wealthier – they tended to remain more or less at the same state they were in between the time following a person's birth and his death.

A person born into a society, almost anywhere on Earth, never knew a different life style. Societies, in an economic sense, were stagnant. With the minor exceptions of temporary changes in their prosperity, which raised living standards if there was a good run of harvests, or rich pickings from the plunder of neighbours, most societies experienced, in its acutest form, the central and oldest economic problem – how to survive, procreate and continue. Civilisations came and went, some glorious and remembered by their buildings, roads and other manufactured items which survive, some remembered for their literature and law-making and others remembered only by the cruelty of their deeds; but for the overwhelming majority of all of the peoples of the Earth, life remained harsh and insecure.

For the minority, the leaders, the rulers, the intellectuals, a few priests and poets, and their immediate families, what they experienced remained for the rest of the human race only a promise, and a pretty far-fetched one at that.

For thousands of years it was thus. Despite having made major discoveries of human intelligence – speech (followed by written language), the wheel, fire, mathematics, processed metals, grain and animal husbandry, fortification, sea travel, and such like – no civilisation passed beyond the limits of its own extravagances (and the bad tempers of its wars) to raise itself above its steady state of stagnation. And so it was for twenty thousand years, until, that is, the middle of the seventeenth century in Europe.

I do not intend to develop a history of the rise of modern society from its earliest beginnings in Europe, nor to trace it to its origins in the societies of Egypt, Babylon, India and China many centuries previously. My point is that within the past four hundred years a significant change has taken place in the course of human development and, barring the final extravagance of nuclear war, it shows every sign of continuing into the future for as long as we can perceive, and this significant change can be summed up in Smith's inquiry: nations, at first imperceptibly and then perceptibly, began to get wealthier and this growth in their wealth has continued at a steady rate for more than two hundred years.

The gradual rise in prosperity has not been confined to a small minority. True, a minority has become richer than its predecessors ever dreamed of, but the vast majority of people who live in the modern societies of the industrialised, or industrialising, part of the Earth, have also grown richer, and much richer than even their ancestors ever dreamed of becoming.

For much of Europe, North America, Australasia, parts of the Middle East, parts of Asia and South America, the improvement in living standards has been highly visible. To put a European peasant in the thirteenth century back to the living standards of his predecessor in the tenth century would hardly have made much material difference to him or his family (assuming we avoided plague years!). To put a factory worker in France today back to the living standards of his grandfather – or even his father – would cause anguish, and a very real material deprivation, precisely because his family's circumstances have altered for the better so dramatically in the past forty years alone.

To say that nations have grown wealthier is not to say that they have become happier or that these are better times in a moral sense. The economist, looking at the vast changes in the wealth of nations, is concerned with the economic aspects of these changes and not with moral precepts.

Smith accepted that improvements in a nation's wealth were on the whole good for the people in the nation. He noted that 'barbarian societies' (those which, in his view, had not yet developed economically) made bad neighbours for wealthy and opulent societies, and were more than likely to cause trouble and threaten wars in pursuit of plunder. For this reason he advocated that an opulent nation should prudently prepare to defend itself ('defence is more important than opulence' he suggested) against a neighbour's depredations.

This drew Smith to a discourse on the proper role of government in an opulent society, though on the whole he thought it best if a society minimised the role of government, and allowed its people a generous freedom to operate in all spheres of economic life. The debate continues today about the proper balance between the functions of a government (confined by Smith to defence, education and some public works) and the freedom of its citizens to engage in trade, business and manufacturing.

The governments of modern states are far more significant economically than they were in Smith's day, and they are far more prone to intervene in economic affairs than he advocated they should be. The wealthier a nation has become the more importance it has attached to the role of government (though you should note that it does not follow that merely increasing the role of government makes a nation more wealthy – in fact the evidence often demonstrates the contrary!). Whereas in Smith's time, and for many decades after, states concerned themselves virtually only with the business of war and internal law and order, gradually they have taken on more roles of an economic character as they have grown richer. They instituted road and transport systems, established public utilities such as gas and electricity supplies and post offices, and gradually moved into running major industrial undertakings (railways, shipyards, airlines and so on). They have also set up nationwide systems of education, and have undertaken health and welfare provision.

Public expenditures, as a proportion of all expenditures in an economy, are in most modern societies in excess of 40 per cent of the total (and in many countries they are even higher). The impact of these important roles for the state are of great interest, and the subject of intense debate, among economists. In the newly created states of the post-1945 decades, the state generally assumed a much larger role in these societies than it had done during comparable periods of economic development in the more advanced economies of Europe and North America. There is no doubt that as these economies develop – get wealthier! – their states will assume even greater roles, if only because the assumption of responsibility for national education, health and social security systems imposes heavy financial burdens that only a state can undertake.

Perhaps I should be a little more specific about the meaning of the concept of the wealth of a nation. So far I have tried to demonstrate what it is by talking about it in the context of events about which you will probably know something. Defining concepts in economics can be like the definition of a camel; it is rather difficult to be precise about a camel, other than to assert that you will know one when you see one. Likewise with a nation's wealth: you may not be sure exactly what is at issue in comparing a wealthy with a poor nation, but you will instinctively know the difference if you move from one to the other.

To get at the definition of the wealth of a nation we have to go beyond the mere stocktaking of its treasures and trinkets. Trunks of diamonds, rubies, silver and gold, valued as they are by those who seek them, are not the real wealth of a nation. For this we have to look for its capacity to feed, clothe, shelter, sustain, and satisfy the needs of its people. In the modern world we are looking at its capacity to provide goods and services, either directly or through trade with others. The more it can meet needs above the level of subsistence (the level at which a person can just sustain life but no more) the richer that society is in the view of an economist.

In a monetary world (and much of the Earth today operates under various monetary systems, hence the interest of economists in money – what it is, whence it comes and what happens to it) the economic capacity of a society can be valued in money terms (eg., dollars, pounds, yen or francs) and we can compare one society's wealth with another's by the money value of what each produces. But it is not the monetary value that is decisive: it is the real goods and services at a society's disposal that determines how rich it is compared with others.

Comparing the money values of each society's output of goods and services enters economics under the title of *national income accounting*, a wholly unexciting topic to be sure, but one which we must cover to get a comprehensive view of macroeconomics.

You will have noted (and if you have not, look back over the previous pages) that I have introduced several topics that interest economists (without at this stage explaining them) and which I can disclose to you now as being items selected from a much larger check-list of topics that make up the subject of macroeconomics.

I have mentioned the role of money, the measurement of wealth, the proportion of public expenditure, taxation, trade, welfare payments and so on. To these we can add topics such as the price level, the rate of inflation, and the growth in national income. All these are the topics of macroeconomics, especially when we refer to them in the *aggregate*, in their totals, and how they interact with each other. Macroeconomics is about economics as seen in the whole. It is about the wealth of the nation, and not just the individual, be he ever so rich. It is about *managing* the economy – the 'commanding heights' – and about which policies are best pursued by the government to attain *national* objectives, and which are best left to the individual to pursue to satisfy *personal* preferences. It is, in sum, about the most suitable economic environment that will permit the economic life of the community, and the individuals who make up that community, to flourish.

Chapter 2

Measuring economic activity

THE IDEA THAT THE DIVERSE LIVES AND BEHAVIOURS of people can be aggregated in some way to present a 'picture' of a society at a moment in time is relatively new. It coincides with the development of the science of economics, and, as an idea, it has grown into a veritable industry; thousands of statisticians pore over numbers, representing the actions of millions of people going about their daily business.

The leap from the idea of measuring a leading family's wealth and social position by the possessions it held (in some societies measured by the castles and lands it possessed, in others by the size of its flocks, or even the number of camels, servants, slaves, and soldiers which it had at its disposal), to the idea of estimating the total wealth of the nation by adding together (aggregating) the wealth of each individual in the entire population, took a long time to occur to those rulers and governments who were most likely to be interested in how each one's nation compared in wealth with that of rivals and neighbours.

The wealth of a nation is a measure of its relative strength, its capacity to influence others and its ability to endure privation in the pursuit of national interest. The warring kingdoms of seventeenth and eighteenth century Europe went about their conflicts largely ignorant of how a neighbour's wealth compared with their own, and, not knowing this crucial information, often made misjudgements in settling on alliances, and, almost always, made misjudgements about their capacity to enforce their writs beyond their established borders. The result was a long record of strife in Europe, not much different in scale from what has been experienced in the Third World since the end of the 1939–45 World War (of the 132 wars since 1945, 129 have taken place in the Third World, and have killed about 20 million people).

This is not to say that there would have been no warlike strife if the kings, princes and presidents of their day had known accurately the exact disposition of material strengths between themselves and their 'enemies'. It can be asserted, however, with a degree of confidence, that if they had avoided the obvious mistakes of assuming themselves to be stronger than they were, they might have been more careful about indulging in military adventures against opponents who were in fact stronger, and therefore more endurable, than they believed them to be, and they might also have avoided some of the more provocative of their political alliances with states which were in fact weaker than they had thought.

The first statistician of a nation's wealth was an Englishman by the name of Sir William Petty (1623–87), who combined a lifetime of service to the state (first, under Oliver Cromwell, England's military dictator, and then under King Charles II) with a dedication to personal enrichment by many, including corrupt, means.

Petty's contribution to macroeconomics was not fully appreciated at the time – after all, nobody thought that the study of an economy was possible, let alone worthwhile, before the seventeenth century and for a long time afterwards. But crude as his first calculations were, they nevertheless laid a basis for further scientific enquiry and improvement, and these researches, over the centuries, have produced sets of data about national economic life that are as accurate as we are likely to get.

Petty set out to establish that the King could raise a much greater revenue from taxation (and thus sustain a larger and more powerful military force) than he had achieved to date. Coming after the bitter, violent and disruptive years of the Cromwellian dictatorship (from which Petty had made a small personal fortune as a state administrator in Ireland), the idea that England was not a weakened and wasted power must have struck his contemporaries as a novel, if not naive one. Certainly, England's rivals in France, the Netherlands and elsewhere, believed it was weaker as a result of the Civil War, and, indeed, we know that the King of France was personally offended by Petty's notion that England was not weaker but stronger than it had been before Cromwell's republic. The French king's attitude is an example, common through all the ages, of an economic conclusion being deduced from a political conviction; in his case that only absolutist monarchy was synonymous with economic strength, and England, having overthrown its monarchy under Cromwell, was necessarily bound to be poorer as a result.

Petty's method of estimating the national wealth of England (at that time not joined with Scotland to form the United Kingdom) was essentially a simple one: he made the assumption that annual income is the equivalent of annual expenditure; if we know what people spend, then we know what they have earned, assuming that savings are small and can be disregarded.

By estimating what it cost, as a bare minimum, to sustain a person each day (for 'food, housing, clothes and other necessaries'), it was possible to sum together all the expenditures of all households and arrive at a total for the kingdom. Petty calculated England's national expenditure, and thereby its income, for a population estimated to be six million people, as £42 million. He did a similar calculation for France, and asserted that England was richer, because, though England was smaller in population compared with France (even after adding in the populations of Scotland, Ireland and the American colonies) it was still richer because its people were more productive.

You should be able to spot one weakness in Petty's method of estimating a country's national income. Apart from the unreliability of seventeenth century population estimates, Petty assumed that every man, woman and child had the *same average daily expenditure* of 4.5 pence a day, or £6 13s 4d a year. Not even in Petty's day could that have been a safe assumption; some were richer than others, and a few (including Petty) grossly so.

It is no good calculating the national income of a modern developing country by multiplying the population by the daily expenditure needed to sustain body and soul together. This would give a wholly inaccurate estimate of the actual national expenditure of a country. For a start – apart from the uncertainties regarding the size of the population in many countries – we know by simple observation that there are vast inequalities in family incomes in developing countries and we also know that there are substantial variations in the expenditure needs of rural subsistence farmers compared with those of urban industrial workers.

Hence, while Petty's estimates were a step forward from what had been undertaken before him (normally, how many soldiers the state could field was the only measure of a country's strength), we must accept that there was still a long way to go before national income estimates were to become accurate rather than fanciful.

It did not take long before somebody else took up where Petty left off. Gregory King (1648–1712) was a totally different civil servant from the unscrupulous and corrupt Petty. He had an unassuming post in the heraldry office, which dispensed heraldic designs to knights and lords of the kingdom. As a result, no doubt because of his skills in the minutiae of heraldic symbolism, which combined artistic skill with prodigious attention to detail (an inheritance could fall on whether a shield was crossed twice or thrice, or a lion had four or five twirls on its mane), King was also a map maker and a surveyor, and could also offer his services as an engraver.

In keeping with his lowly role, King was also self-effacing to the degree that he did not publish his national income statistics in his own name but gave permission to Charles Davenant to publish extracts from them. It was not until 1802 that the full version of King's work was published and his genius recognised.

Perhaps it was inevitable that King would look at the problem of estimating the national income in a different way from that used by Petty. King was, after all, very conscious of rank and status in England. What is heraldry but a pictorial statement of a person's status? Hence, King set about estimating the national income of England by means of a social and economic stratification of its various classes, from 'Temporal lords', through 'Bishops', 'Knights', 'Gentlemen', 'Shopkeepers', and thence to 'Common seamen', 'Labouring people', 'Paupers' and 'Common soldiers', and, finally, to 'Vagrants'. He estimated the number of families for each rank, the number in each family, their yearly income as a family and their family income per head, and added together the entire lot to arrive at a sum, not too far away from Petty's, of £43,505,800 for the year 1688.

It is by looking at *how* these early pioneers of national income analysis went about their work, that you will appreciate modern approaches to essentially the same task.

Petty estimated expenditure needs per day and then multiplied this number by an estimate of the population, taking no account of the very great differences in family circumstances; King started with family financial circumstances and estimated how many families were in each category, and then multiplied these together to get a total income for the entire kingdom.

Today, we go about it differently. Whereas both Petty and King had no means of counting every household in the country, and had to rely on their estimates of these, modern states conduct regular censuses and do know the number of people in the country and also have detailed knowledge of the number of people in each household.

But the improvement in national statistics has gone much further in almost all dimensions. Details are collected of the wages paid to every employee, the taxation paid to the government, the interest paid on all loans, the rent paid for all property and the profits earned by each business, be they one-person shops or multinational enterprises.

Governments collect statistics on the number of people who undertake paid employment, what kinds of work they do, the nature of the activity of the firms they work for. The number of unemployed people who want to work, but who do not yet have a job, is also counted, plus what kinds of jobs they are seeking and for how long they have been seeking them (and, also, age, sex and residence).

In many countries, the government requires firms to remit details of their output, by the month or quarter, and these are aggregated to produce industry or service sector totals. In this way, the government can produce details of the types of economic activity undertaken within its territory.

By requiring details of all exports, information is collected on what the country is exporting (and to which countries), and, through its controls of the customs service, it can also check on what the country is importing (and from which countries). The total output of the country, including exports, can be compared with the total consumption of the country, including imports, which gives a clearer, and more detailed, picture of the economic activity of a country than was attempted by either Petty or King.

With millions of people involved in economic activity, especially in the more populous countries, it is not practicable, and is prohibitively expensive, to collect details of weekly, monthly and quarterly expenditure. In this case, sampling is undertaken, in which a small proportion of the population is randomly chosen and required to answer a questionnaire on what they have spent their incomes. By selecting samples from each household type (single person, married couple, married couple with one child, single person with one child, and so on), estimates for each household type and each income level can be made, and a fairly accurate picture of household expenditure can be assembled.

The proportions of each household type in the population, and the income distribution from the very poorest to the very richest, are known to be fairly stable between census years, and it is a matter of arithmetic (normally undertaken by computers) to work out the totals for the country as a whole. Unlike Gregory King, who had to guess the numbers and income for each social class, modern census and expenditure surveys can produce accurate and reliable estimates which are suitable for policy making by government agencies.

I do not want to leave you with the impression that today's national income statistics are always accurate to the point where they cannot be improved. This would be altogether a wrong impression, especially in certain countries where, perhaps because of a poverty of resources to devote to the collection of statistical data, or because of disruptions caused by war and civil war, or because of other pressing priorities, there are many gaps in data collection, and in these circumstances there is much to be desired in the way the data is collected and processed.

In addition, there are problems for statistical work created by a desire on the part of some governments to 'massage' the data to produce wholly undeserved political impressions. Some governments might want to impress others by the progress they appear to be making in their national targets – thus justifying the politics or the attitudes of the leaders of the government, or they may wish to continue to qualify for certain forms of aid by giving the impression that their country is worse off than it is in fact – thus playing on the conscience of richer members of the United Nations.

Apart from these possibilities, there is much that remains controversial in national income statistics, both at the conceptual level – can, for example, a country's welfare be measured by the economic value of its output? – and at the practical level – can we rely on these figures, and the way they were collected and computed, to be representative of the economic values we want to measure?

We shall return to these issues as we go along, and while you should be aware that controversies exist about this or that system of national income analysis, you ought also to be aware that, in the main, and certainly in the richer industrialised countries, national income accounts are fairly reliable and representative of a country's economic circumstances.

Chapter 3

Circular flows of economic activity

ONE THING YOU WILL HAVE TO BECOME ACCUSTOMED TO IN ECONOMICS is the use of what we call *models*. They appear in almost all aspects of economics. It is doubtful whether an economic text could ever be written – and understood! – that did not rely upon models of one kind or another to explain a particular point or a relevant relationship.

What is a model? The best way to think about a model is to consider one with which you are bound to be familiar: a street map of a city you visit or in which you live. The map is a graphical model of an actual place. It does not go into every detail of the city. In fact, most maps have only the outlines of named streets, and show no details of the buildings or other features of the city.

Depending upon the purpose of the map – to identify street names and their location, for example – as little detail as possible is shown in order to simplify your use of it. If you want additional details, you must purchase a more detailed map, but it is certain that not even the most detailed map – one showing how hilly the city is, which way the traffic flows, and the outline shapes of the buildings and so on – would be other than representative (i.e. a model) of the city to which it applies.

Maps summarise significant and relevant information and suppress less significant and less relevant information. That is an important characteristic of a model: it eliminates minute detail in order to concentrate attention upon essential features that are required for the specific purpose for which it is constructed.

You may be familiar with other models, such as scale drawings of a building, the floor plans of an apartment block, the drawings of a machine part that are used by those who manufacture it, the models of automobiles and aircraft (you will see the latter displayed by travel agents who want to impress potential clients with modern aircraft fleet), maps of a railway system showing the stations along the line, and of a country's road system. Government agencies regularly update maps of property boundaries to show the exact boundaries of what people own.

Models, therefore, are abstract representations, and because economists wish to eliminate a lot of detail, they use models to make sure that their attention is concentrated on, and only on, the features of the economy, or the part of the economy they are studying. By eliminating inessential details, we are not diverted into considering aspects of social life that are not relevant to economics, though they may be relevant to sociology, psychology, history or whatever.

The best way to grasp something new is to have it demonstrated to you, and we shall therefore apply what has been said about models to a particular example. Time spent studying this first model will pay large dividends later on when you tackle more complex models common to macroeconomics.

So far we have mentioned households, business firms, and governments, and we have alluded, without going into too much detail, to the economic functions of each of them. It is time to begin to open up these institutions to further study and to look for economic links between them.

First, we shall take a look at the relationships between, and the economic purpose of, two main sectors of an economy, namely, those of *households* and *businesses*. Later on, we shall add complexity to this simple economic model by introducing two other sectors, *government* and *foreign trade*.

Households can consist of one or several persons. In the real world we normally associate a household with a family – everybody in the household is related in some way to everybody else in the household. Now we know from observation that this is not always the case. Some families do not live together (they could be divorced, or separated temporarily by work or study), and some people who live together are not members of the same family (they could be fellow students staying together while they are at college, each fully intending to go his or her own way when they graduate). But in common with the use of models, we exclude all these considerations and concentrate upon the broadly defined household as the place where the output of the economy is *consumed*.

In our simple model, businesses are similarly considered in their simplest form. In this model, it is of no consequence whether the business is a one-person shop, an owner-driver taxi, or whether it is a multi-person enterprise with branches all over the country. In this simple model, it does not affect the relationship of business activity to that of households if one or hundreds or thousands of people are employed in the business. All businesses simply undertake *production* activity and supply *output* to households for them to *consume*.

Our interest in the activities of businesses as producers, and of households as consumers, is to highlight the relationship between the two, so that we can see the way in which business output becomes household consumption. If we can understand how this basic relationship operates, we ought to be able, in principle, to add complexity to the simple model and study more complicated relationships between businesses and households.

Let us begin analysing Fig. 1 (see page 22), and see what we can get out of our first simple model of an economic relationship, that between the aggregate of all households and the aggregate of all businesses.

22 · Circular flows of economic activity

The box on the left is labelled 'households' and the box on the right is labelled 'businesses'. Neither category shows any detail about what kinds of households they are, nor what kinds of businesses are operating in this model of an economy.

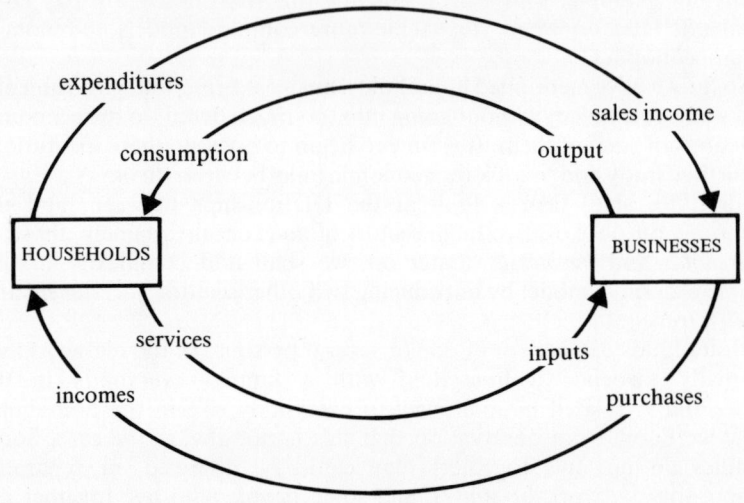

FIG. 1: **Relationships between households and businesses**

Because we know that they have a relationship, we want to represent it in the model. If they did not have a relationship, households would be unable to consume that which is produced, and businesses would be unable to produce that which is destined to be consumed.

In a modern economy, businesses purchase *inputs* and transform them into *outputs*, which they sell to households. These inputs can be the labour services of employees, the use of buildings or land owned by households, or the borrowing of money from households to purchase labour, machinery, raw materials, and other services.

Households sell the services of their members (mainly their labour services, but also property they own, and financial services such as loans of money) to businesses. For these services they receive payments (wages for labour, rents for property, interest on loans, profits from owning businesses etc.) which they use to buy the output of businesses.

In Fig. 1 the inside circle shows households supplying *services* which are the *inputs* of businesses, and businesses supplying *output* which is the *consumption* of households.

In a monetary economy, flows of economic activity are paid for by counter-flows of money. This is shown in the outer circle of Fig. 1. Businesses make purchases (eg. labour services) which become the income of households, and households make expenditures which become the income of businesses.

Circular flows of economic activity · 23

For every supply of something, whether it be a service that a business wishes to purchase, or an output that a household wishes to consume, the principle is the same: cash moves to the sector that supplies what the other sector requires, and what the other sector requires moves to the sector that supplies the cash.

This model shows the *circular flow* of economic activity (goods or services in one direction, earnings in the other direction), and it identifies the basic relationship between households and businesses in a simple economy; each depends upon the other to supply what it requires to continue to function, for without inputs, known as the *factors of production*, the business sector would soon cease to operate, and without output, known as *final goods and services*, the household sector would soon cease to consume.

In this simple model there is no other source for either the inputs of businesses or the consumption of households other than businesses or households, represented in Fig. 1. This might be an obvious point, though judging from remarks made by politicians from time to time, it is not everywhere appreciated. There are no 'bottomless pits', out of which either inputs or outputs can be conjured up to satisfy needs, however worthy. If households do not have services to supply to businesses, or businesses do not have outputs to supply to households, then neither sector can get them from somewhere else.

Economic wealth has to be created by someone; it does not fall like manna from heaven (and even then would still have to be collected and distributed by somebody at some cost in time and effort).

If you are thinking about the possibility of the government supplying inputs or output, or of the country acquiring them from another country, you certainly deserve marks for questioning what you are reading (a sign of a diligent student!), but as I shall show you in the next chapter, neither the existence of governments, nor the possibility of gifts from another country, alters the basic proposition that 'there ain't no such thing as a free lunch', because someone, somewhere, some time, must pay for it either in cash or in kind.

Chapter 4

Government and the circular flow

IT IS FAIRLY COMMON, at least in the country that I live in, to hear people demanding that the government spends more money on this or that – usually either on something that they themselves would benefit from or about which they feel strongly in a moral sense. Thus, we hear, from parents, and people employed as teachers, demands for more money to be spent on education; from patients or the families of patients, and from medical staff, for more money to be spent on hospitals; from military personnel, or those who feel threatened by 'enemies', for more money to be spent on defence; and from employees and their customers, for more subsidies to be given to uneconomic businesses.

It is an almost universal experience for citizens to demand more spending by the government, without in any way making explicit the basic economic truth that more spent on your favourite programme means less spent on somebody else's. The government is seen as the 'bottomless spending pit' of the economy. It is always being called upon to do more, much more than it is doing, and any failure of the government to meet these demands is a clear sign, in the view of many citizens, and certainly their political leaders, that it does not want to do so for one reason or another.

It is not that governments are minor influences on modern economies. They account for large proportions – between 30 and 60 per cent – of the economic activity of modern economies, including those economies that disavow any socialistic intentions. Governments, in the last quarter of the twentieth century, are *big* governments; they wield enormous economic power, employ hundreds of thousands of people, and intervene extensively in the economy.

Hence, the simple model of the economy discussed in Chapter 3 needs to be elaborated, and necessarily made slightly more complex, than the one shown in Fig. 1. We must, for a start, incorporate a government sector in the model, and with this elaboration examine the various relationships of the government to the household and business sectors. But first, we shall examine an economic model of a socialist type of society where the government performs all the activities of the business sector (under a state system of nationalised business), and where the relationship of the household to the government sector replicates in all details that of households to the business sector in a capitalist society.

This is shown in Fig. 2(a) where the right hand box is labelled 'government', instead of 'business'. I shall return to the situation in a capitalist society in a moment.

The household and government sectors are shown in the left and right hand boxes respectively. Again, we are aiming to keep the analysis as simple as possible and, therefore, we are looking for only the most straightforward of the many relationships that exist between the sectors. We are not, for instance, considering political relationships – households in democracies elect the government and all members of a government live in households – nor the legal relationships – governments make laws and households and businesses obey those laws – nor any of the other relationships that exist.

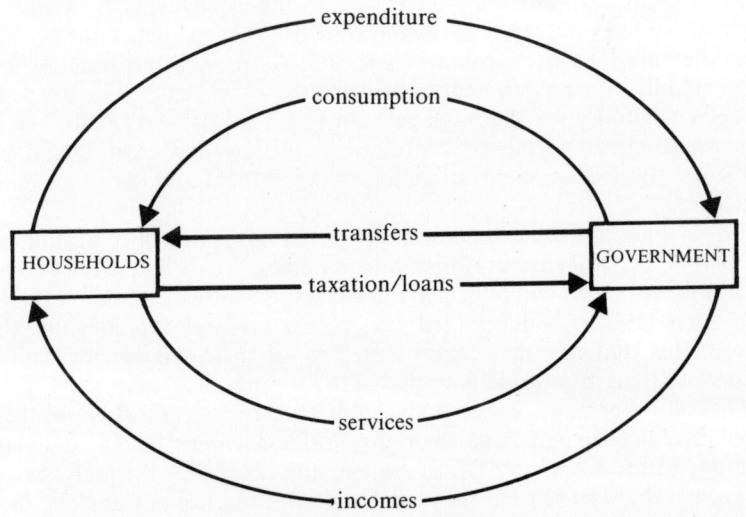

FIG. 2(a): **Relationships between households and government**

The first thing to bear in mind is that governments in themselves do not create anything in an economic sense. They have an economic impact in Fig. 2(a) only because households fund government activities out of taxation, or by means of loans, or through the purchase of output from government-owned businesses. A government may siphon off part of a country's income for its own purposes, and whether these purposes are 'good' or 'bad' does not alter the proposition that they cannot 'create' economic wealth by exercising the function of government alone; to do this they must take over the function of business in Fig. 1.

If they wish to engage in the function of wealth creation they must engage in business activities, either directly through the state ownership of a business, or indirectly through state sponsorship of business. They cannot create wealth merely by legislating for it to be created. Would that they could, for then poverty would have been abolished long ago all over the planet to a chorus of 'ayes' in every legislature in the world!

Governments fund their activities by diverting to their treasuries, in the form of taxation, a proportion of the incomes of their citizens. Taxes are compulsory in every part of the world – not even in the socialist countries, where, in theory, people consciously support state sponsored activities, are taxes left to the voluntary contributions of the masses.

In Fig. 2(a) households contribute compulsory taxation and voluntary savings to the government.

Governments make payments to households in the form of unemployment pay, social security, sickness pay, old age pensions, widows' pensions and such like. These are known collectively as *transfers*.

Individuals in households have title to these payments by virtue of their status (they are temporarily out of work, they are below the poverty line, they are over the retirement age and so on), and not because they have supplied the government with anything, other than, perhaps, proof of their eligibility for the payments. In other words, the entitlement of citizens to these payments is prescribed by law and custom and not because of any economic transaction between them and the government sector.

The economic effect of taxation on households is to reduce the amount of income that they have available to purchase goods and services from government-owned and managed businesses. Because of income taxation, and such taxes as value added tax, petrol tax and capital gains tax, households that pay these taxes have less of their original incomes to dispose of than they would have had in the absence of all taxes.

On the other hand, those households that receive transfer payments from the government have their disposable incomes increased by the amount of the transfers, less, of course, any taxes they themselves must pay when they spend what they receive. In the absence of transfers, these households would necessarily have a lower standard of living if their incomes were not supplemented in this way.

Fig. 2(a) shows the economic relationship between households and government from the economic exchange of labour services, supplied by civil servants who are employed to administer government services and operate its business enterprises. This is perfectly analagous with that of the relationship between a business that purchases inputs and a household that supplies them. In the government's case, households supply labour services in the form of administrative inputs by civil servants in exchange for incomes which are spent on goods and services supplied by government-owned businesses.

In this model, we can conceive of taxes as a purchase by households of government-owned outputs, which the government supplies by purchasing the necessary inputs in the form of labour services from households. Its businesses supply outputs (perhaps in the form of military equipment, for example) which the government uses or, in the case of other goods and services, disposes of them to households according to whatever criteria it chooses, probably on political grounds.

Households purchase those goods and services that are made available for consumption, and pay for them out of their incomes, either earned in exchange for selling their labour services to government-owned enterprises and administrative departments of the state, or from non-economically determined transfers (pensions etc.).

It should be borne in mind, in this model of a socialist economy, that on the basis of experience since 1917, if not in socialist theory, decisions as to the quantity and quality of the goods and services which shall be produced, and their prices, and how much should be paid for labour services (there are no financial services of a free market kind in a socialist economy), and what the levels of taxation should be, and how much, and to whom, all transfer payments should apply, are determined by the government and not by households. This is the single most pertinent difference between a socialist and a capitalist economy. In the latter, decisions are not concentrated in a single sector, but are shared between them, particularly in political democracies where governments are influenced by consumer tastes and expectations.

But what of a capitalist economy that also has a large and important government sector as well as an independent business sector? Can we model this complication in a simple circular flow diagram? Of course!

In Fig. 2(b) (see page 28) the circular flow has been extended to include both a government and a business sector. Once again, we can work our way round the figure to highlight the features of the model (and if you weary at the thought of this, please persevere because it will be more than worth it in the long run).

Households supply government and business with labour services. Civil servants are employed to administer government departments (those immigration officials interrogating you as you try to enter a foreign country, those taxation officials scrutinising your tax returns, those soldiers, airmen and sailors standing guard over your country's frontiers, and those education officials deciding on whether to award you a student's grant, etc.).

In Fig. 2(b) we also allow for those households who supply labour services to operate government-run enterprises (railways, airlines, post offices, nationalised companies and such like). They receive incomes and these are spent on both goods and services supplied by businesses (as in Fig. 1) and those outputs supplied by government departments (official papers, documents and so on) and government-owned enterprises (in many countries, rail travel, telecommunications, etc.).

Households are taxed and also volunteer to lend money to the government (to earn interest), and these funds, plus the earnings from selling government services, constitute the total source of income of the government sector.

Alongside these government/household economic transactions

(basically, taxation, loans and labour services in one direction, and transfers, earnings and government outputs in the other direction), we have the relationship between households and the business sector, as described in Chapter 3.

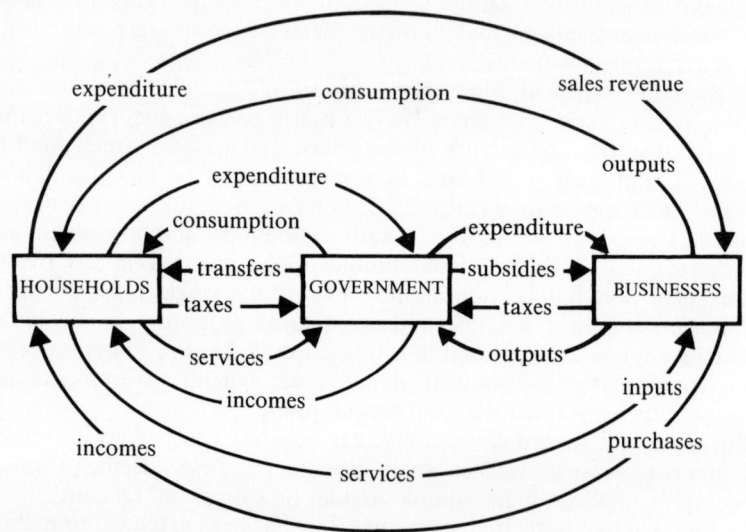

FIG. 2(b): **Relationships between households, government and business**

Households supply labour and other services to businesses and receive wages, interest, rent and profits in return. Wages come from selling labour services, interest from loaning money, rent from letting property, and profits from owning businesses. Businesses sell their final output to households and receive sales revenue in return.

Businesses also have a relationship with the government sector. They pay taxes (output, employment, value added and profit taxes among others) and receive subsidies, for one reason or another (such as to encourage investment in particular regions of the country, to preserve key industries for commercial or political reasons, or to assist with restructuring and change). Governments also buy output from businesses – filing cabinets, word processors, paper clips, buildings, vehicles, tanks, aircraft, frigates, etc.—and for these, businesses receive sales revenue.

Thus, in the mixed capitalist/government economy – the most common type of economy in the richer countries of the world – we have a complex inter-relationship between households, government and businesses.

What the balance between the three sectors should be to achieve the best results is a controversial subject, and one on which you will hear a great deal in your studies of economics and politics.

Some argue that capitalist societies, when left alone by governments, tend to run at a level of activity which leaves spare resources unused, usually labour in the form of unemployment, and that this is an avoidable social waste. Their answer is to increase the role of government-backed enterprise to mop up surplus labour and other resources which otherwise would stand idle.

Others argue that government intervention, by its nature, is bound to be less efficient than activity that is motivated by the prospect of personal gain if the intervenor is right, and the certainty of personal loss if the intervenor is wrong, if only because the individual who makes the decision cares more about the outcome than a civil servant who has the security of a job for life.

If there is manifest wastage of economic resources (labour, financial services and productive capacity), there is a source of potential anxiety among those who want their country to be economically powerful. If, on the other hand, there is vast incompetence and visible wastage of economic resources because government officials spend unwisely and invest recklessly (even for the best of possible motives), this also weakens the economy and exposes it to political extremism, and associated disagreeable threats to peace and security.

Nobody yet, however, has found an answer to the dilemma of choosing between the alternative policies of benign neglect or benign interference, without risking consequential damage to the economic fabric of society. A Nobel Prize in Economics (and, in view of its contribution to human happiness, probably a simultaneous Nobel Prize for Peace!) awaits the first person definitively to solve this dilemma.

Chapter 5

Foreign trade and the circular flow

ALL COUNTRIES IN THE MODERN WORLD trade with somebody, if not everybody. There are all kinds of (good) reasons for international trade (taken up in Part IV). Not the least of them is that it enables a country to gain access to goods and services otherwise denied to it, or, if not denied in principle, at least denied in practical terms because of the comparative expense of producing goods and services themselves instead of importing them more cheaply.

By way of illustration, Adam Smith pointed out that it might be possible to produce French-style claret (wine) in Scotland by means of a system of 'hothouses'. The expense of constructing hothouses would be occasioned by the Scottish weather (which for those of you unfamiliar with Scotland, can best be described as very 'unclaret type' weather, to put it gently!). Smith's point was not that it was, perhaps, technically infeasible to replicate French claret in this way, but that it was totally unnecessary, for if the Scots wished to consume French claret they could do so by importing it from France and paying for it by exporting Scottish products in exchange.

Trade widens opportunities for consumption beyond those goods which a single nation can produce on its own. Coffee from South America can be exchanged for computers from Europe; oil from Saudi Arabia can be paid for with aircraft from North America; television sets from Japan can be paid for by oil from Kuwait; pineapples from Jamaica can be paid for by automobiles from Germany, and so on. That which a country is good at producing, whether by virtue of its geology, its geography, its technical skills, or because of its outright good fortune, can be exchanged for the products of another country.

How then can we integrate a trade sector into the model of an economy described in Chapter 4 with household, government and business sectors? First, we should add a foreign trade sector into the original model of Chapter 3, it always being wiser to take a gentle approach when making models more complex. When this has been understood, we can then integrate the trade model into the three-sector model of Chapter 4.

In Fig. 3(a), we have three sectors, households in the left hand box, businesses in the right hand box, and foreign trade in the upper box. The relationships between households and businesses are the same as those described in Chapter 3. Households in Fig. 3(a) do not sell their services to the foreign trade sector, nor do they receive incomes from it (though in more complex models we could show households selling their financial services to foreign businesses and receiving in return repatriated incomes from them).

The relationship between households and the foreign trade sector in Fig. 3(a) is confined to the purchase of foreign goods by households for personal consumption (Japanese television sets and video recorders, or German motor vehicles, or British clothes and books), and is shown as expenditures on imports. From the point of view of the foreign traders, these transactions appear as receipts from exports to households.

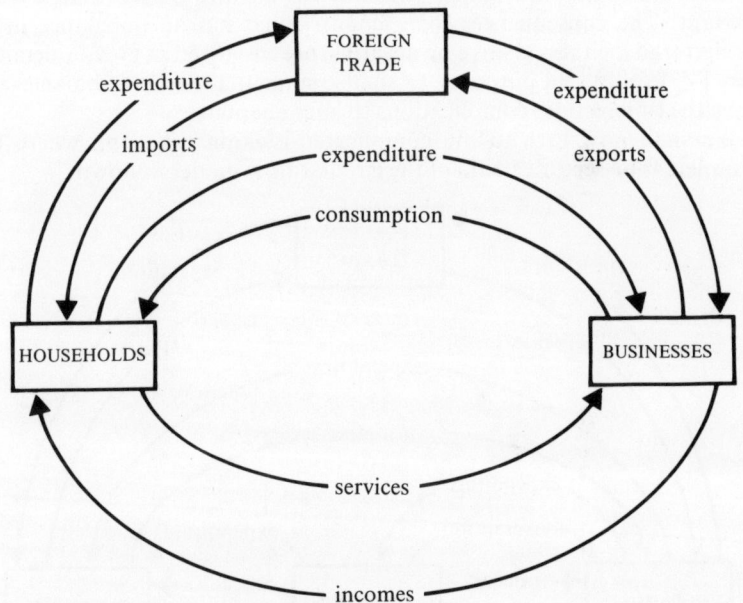

FIG. 3(a): **Foreign trade and the circular flow**

Naturally, by spending some proportion of household income, earned from selling services to businesses, on imports of foreign goods and services, households are diverting some of their income from domestic to foreign businesses. This means that having created domestic output, by transforming their inputs through business activity, households are not buying it all back in their consumption expenditures. Domestic businesses, in the absence of some other source of sales revenue, must therefore have a surplus of unsold output, and would face a serious problem if this continued. They would have to curtail their domestic output to match the amount of household expenditure spent on domestically-produced goods and services. Curtailing domestic output would reduce household

32 · Foreign trade and the circular flow

incomes by the amount of labour and other services businesses would dispense with.

The prospect of international trade means that domestic businesses have an outlet for output that is unsold to domestic households. In Fig. 3(*a*) domestic businesses export some of their output to foreign traders, who import it for sale to their countries' households. To pay for these imports, foreign traders make foreign expenditures, which become foreign sales receipts for domestic businesses.

Now as long as the proportion of household income spent on foreign imports is roughly equal to the value of domestic output sold to foreign traders, a country will remain, broadly, in balance on its foreign trade account. The consequences for a country that has an imbalance in its foreign trade, either positive or negative, are discussed in greater detail in Part IV. For present purposes we shall assume that there is a balance and leave the (interesting) complications to later chapters.

We shall now turn to the complicated-looking Fig. 3(*b*), where the complete four-sector version of the circular flow model is shown.

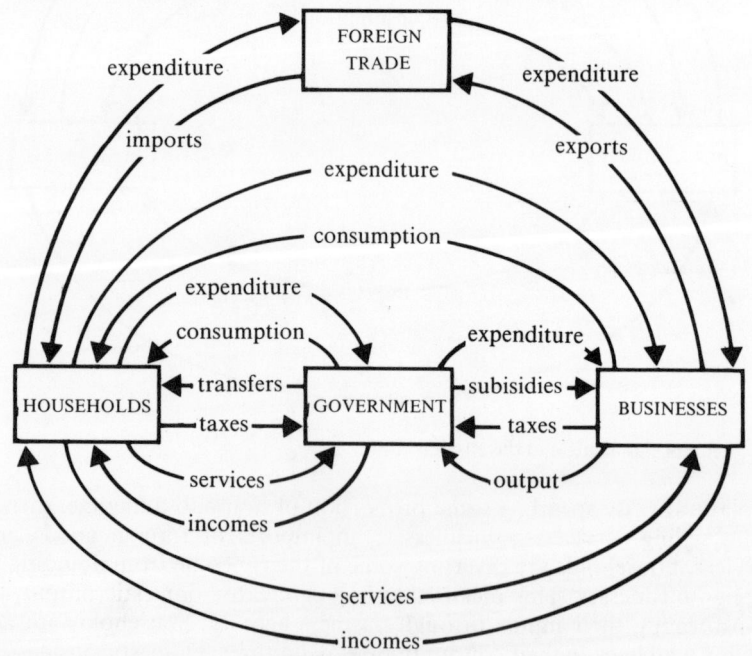

FIG. 3(*b*): **Foreign trade and the circular flow – influence of government considered**

It is always a good idea to look at a new diagram much as you would a picture in a gallery – 'stand back' and look over it for a while before homing in on individual parts of it. Another tip, which applies to all graphical models in economics, is not to try and 'read' the model from the text, but to take out a pencil and paper and draw the model yourself as the text explains each part. That way you will get a feel for how it is constructed and what each part means (just as, with mathematical calculations, it helps to 'work through' the steps in the argument to understand what is actually going on).

Here we have the relationships between the household, government, business and foreign trade sectors shown together. Visually, it looks a lot more fearsome than it is in fact. If you have followed the exposition of the previous versions of the model, you should have no difficulty in putting the elements together into one diagram.

Basically, the model shows the relationships of households with the other sectors, though for the sake of clarity I have not shown any relationships between the government and foreign trade sectors. This is a gross simplification, because governments clearly do have a foreign trade relationship. For example, governments import goods and services from foreign countries (military aircraft for instance) and they pay money over to foreign governments (reparations for war damage, economic aid for development), to foreign businesses (purchases of foreign military products) and to foreign households (pensions paid to overseas residents). These transactions, important as they are, have been left out of consideration in this version of the model.

Households sell their services to businesses or to the government, and receive wages in return. In addition, households, by virtue of their current status, may receive transfer payments. Whatever the sources of their income, households spend it on goods and services supplied by domestic businesses and from foreign traders, for whom these expenditures constitute income.

Governments purchase goods and services from businesses, and subsidise business activities with grants and allowances. They receive taxes from businesses, and these help to fund government activities. Businesses sell a proportion of their outputs to foreign traders, from whom they receive foreign sales revenue, while households spend a proportion of their incomes on imports, creating export revenue for foreign traders.

Assuming everything is in equilibrium, i.e., the sum of all incomes equals the sum of all expenditures between sectors, the model will represent a stable economy, where the value of business output equals the sales revenue from domestic and foreign sales, where the incomes of all households equals the expenditures of all households (we assume in this model no savings), and where the taxation and borrowing of government equals its expenditures on transfers to, and purchase of labour services from, households, and subsidies to, and expenditures on supplies from, all businesses.

Fig. 3(b) is a relatively simple model of an economy. It does not by any means represent the complexities of a real economy. It does not consider such an important economic activity as savings, except where they appear in the forms of active loans to government or business, and also it is entirely static. No discrepancies between one time period and another are shown, and everything is assumed to be in balance at the moment that the model is drawn.

These features make Fig. 3(*b*) wholly unrealistic, but nevertheless we have a representative model of an economy that illustrates how some important activities interact with each other. And, after all, that is the purpose of a model: to elucidate certain features of a relationship even at the cost of sacrificing other important features, which can be tackled only by recourse to models of greater complexity (mathematical models, for example).

Having set the scene with these simple models we can now pass on to look at the derivation of national income accounts in some greater detail, and in doing so, we can become more precise about some of the concepts we have been using.

Chapter 6

Components of the national income

SO FAR I HAVE DISCUSSED SIMPLE MODELS of an economy in order to highlight some important features of the relationships between the basic sectors, households, businesses, government and foreign trade. I have also used various terms, such as 'consumption', 'output', 'inputs', 'factor services', 'sales revenues' and so on, without precisely defining what these terms mean. I have left you to conjure up a 'common sense' meaning for these terms.

It is now necessary for us to go into the meanings of these, and several other terms, as I intend to use them in an introduction to the subject of national income accounting (which I warn you now, is hardly the most exciting topic in macroeconomics!). But this excursion is unavoidable if we are to appreciate the significance of the national income accounts in explaining a country's economic activity, and its prospects for economic growth.

We start with the measure of the total output of an economy – known as the *Gross National Product* (GNP), or *Gross National Income* (which, for reasons too obscure to develop here, is universally known by the symbol Y). In due course we shall see that the GNP and the Y are measures of the same thing, and may be used interchangeably depending upon context and convenience.

The total output of an economy (let's call it Y, and fall in with a convention adopted by economists many years ago), consists of certain activities that can be distinguished because they involve decisions by different groups of people. We have already been introduced to them, in one form, in our simple models of the earlier chapters, namely: household *consumption*, business *investment*, government *expenditures* and the foreign trade *balance*.

Beginning with household *consumption* (given the symbol C by economists) we can define this as all those activities that consist of the purchase in markets of goods and services that yield direct personal satisfaction.

For example, a household purchases food, which yields personal satisfaction, for without food the members of the household would starve and die. Without clothes they could freeze from exposure (or suffer from sunburn), as well as cause embarrassment to themselves (for we do not all have the human form of Adonis or Aphrodite!) and offend the social conventions of neighbours. Without somewhere for shelter, we would lead a miserable existence, being cold and unprotected at night, and perhaps dirty and soaking wet in turns. Hence, if we can, we purchase or rent accommodation.

That proportion of the output of a society that goes towards the direct satisfaction of our personal needs, we call *consumption*. In modern societies, personal consumption can account for up to 60 per cent of the total ouput of an economy, and it could be said (and was said by Adam Smith among others) that personal consumption is the sole purpose of economic activity in a free society (in contrast with that of a slave society, where the purpose of consumption is to sustain people solely for work).

If we sum together the expenditures of individual households, we arrive at the total expenditure of households on consumption, and this provides us with information on the largest single component of national income.

As you study economics, you will soon cease to be surprised that there are complicating issues at stake when we attempt to measure what appears to be a straightforward concept such as household consumption. Unfortunately, not all expenditure on goods and services for personal consumption is consumed at once, or even within a year.

Take, for example, the purchase of a house or a motor vehicle. The house will provide shelter for many years (if it doesn't, you have bought the wrong house!), and the motor vehicle should last for some time to come (unless you were sold a wreck). Neither of these goods (and many others we could have chosen for illustration, such as durable goods like washing machines, television sets, cookers, refrigerators) is consumed by the household immediately, or even in the relatively short term.

People expect a house to provide shelter for a long time to come, and even if they do not intend to live in the house for very long themselves, they will expect to be able to sell the house to somebody else who will consume its services for many years into the future. A motor vehicle should also last a long time, and the fact that a motor vehicle has a second-hand re-sale price suggests that its transport services are not exhausted by its first owner.

This presents us with a statistical problem. If we are counting as personal consumption those goods and services that provide immediate satisfaction to households, how do we treat those household purchases that clearly have a service life longer than is warranted by the description 'immediate satisfaction'?

The short answer is that we don't distinguish between household purchases that produce immediate satisfaction in consumption (for example, ice-cream, newspapers, a cool drink) and those that provide regular services, spread over many years (for example, houses or transport).

To attempt to distinguish between these two categories of consumption would involve such complicated problems for statisticians that the resultant information would hardly be worth while collecting, given what it would cost to collect it, and would probably not be usable anyway, given the time needed to do so. Hence, for purposes of the national accounts, we treat all household expenditures within the time period (usually a year), whether on perishable food or durable kitchen units, as immediate consumption (C) no matter how long it takes in fact for the household to consume the items concerned.

Our second category of economic activity was that of businesses, and you may have noticed that in this chapter I referred to the economic activity of business as *investment*. This needs to be explained because it is the first reference I have made to the activity of investment.

Businesses hire labour services (for wages), and apply these services to bought-in raw materials and equipment of one kind or another (which the business either owns or hires) to produce output. Labour services are hired, not owned – employees are not slaves, owned by the employer, but free agents able to sell their labour services to whomsoever wishes to hire them. They go home to their households at the end of each working session and lead their lives free of interference from the businesses that employ them.

Can the same be said of the equipment (machinery and such like) of a business? In the main, the business will *own* its buildings and equipment; it can dispose of them as it pleases, either by selling or hiring them to another business, or by letting them stand idle and unused. Even if it hires all its equipment from another business, it will still *manage* (i.e. be in charge of and responsible for) its hired assets.

Likewise with its material inputs, be they uncooked food for the restaurant, metals in an unworked-up state, semi-manufactured parts which it will assemble, or paper for its computer print-outs. These are owned by the business, and remain under the direct control of the managers of the business, while they await to be processed and prepared for sale to customers.

Economists consider certain activities of a business, like the acquisition of newly produced capital equipment (machines, etc.), as the act of *investment*.

This must be distinguished from a common idea of investment, often used in a popular sense, and sometimes by accountants, when we talk of 'investing in a business', i.e., purchasing shares in it for money. The economic meaning of business investment is the acquisition of capital goods as inputs to produce output.

The sum of all newly-produced capital goods in a period of time is known as *gross investment*. Some proportion of these newly-produced capital goods will be purchased to replace worn out machinery that has been used up in previous time periods while producing previous outputs. After deducting this replacement investment from gross investment we have the *net* addition to existing investment, or, as it is known, *net investment*.

As we shall see, this latter type of investment is of crucial importance in economic policy making, because an economy that manages to add to its stock of currently existing capital goods by net investment, over and above the capital goods it uses up, is expanding its capacity to produce future outputs, or, in short, is creating conditions for economic growth.

We now have two main categories of economic activity: consumption by households and investment by businesses. The former is treated as if it were consumed immediately, which means it is *not* available for creating future outputs – what is consumed is gone forever, it is a bygone.

Investment is partly a replacement for worn out equipment, and is used up in future time periods to create future output. In other words, investment is a postponement of consumption; it is like the seed corn kept back by the farmer to produce next season's crops.

Consumption is current wealth; investment is the means to create future wealth. If all that is produced is consumed, and none invested, there is no future at all. If farmers eat their seed corn, they have no tomorrow, for they will starve without a means of producing corn for next season's harvest. If an economy does not invest to replace its stock of wealth-creating capital, it will eventually die as its capital goods are worn out.

Governments spend their income from taxation and borrowing, and this constitutes another major component of the GNP. It is generally designated by the symbol G.

There are two main features of government expenditure that are worth noting here (and remembering later in discussions on economic policy). The first has already been alluded to, namely, that the government's income derives from the household and business sectors; no government creates wealth; all are in a dependent relationship in an economy. Governments take purchasing power from the household and business sectors and use it to purchase goods and services in accordance with their political objectives and priorities.

This raises the second main feature of government expenditures, namely that what it supplies is not, in the main, sold in the market place, and, therefore, cannot be valued by the prices that people are prepared to pay for it. Defence expenditure is not sold in the form of military power to the citizenry, nor is law and order, justice, and the road system. These are paid out of income taken from the public and, with minor exceptions (such as some tolls on certain bridges and some inter-city roads), distributed at no charge to the community.

Having paid for defence out of taxation, we do not expect to have to buy it out of our incomes as well. Once defence is undertaken, we all benefit from its 'output' (security). Indeed, if we were given a choice of paying or not paying for an activity such as defence, would we offer to pay our share, or would we (more likely) rely on others to pay for it, knowing that we cannot be excluded from its benefits once it is provided?

A similar argument supports compulsory taxation to pay for roads, street lighting, refuse collection, and public parks. Once these are provided, the citizenry as a whole benefits from them, whether or not all pay taxes. To exclude some citizens from consuming publicly-provided goods would not only offend the concept of the community that makes up the nation, but would also be impractical, or an unnecessary expense.

Governments purchase considerable quantities of goods and services from the business sector. These are paid for by the government at whatever price they negotiate with the suppliers, and this is the cost which is entered into the national income accounts and not the price at which a market might value the resultant services (hospitals, police forces, etc.).

Finally, we must include the foreign trade sector in the national accounts. If a country exports a proportion of its output, these goods and services are not available for household consumption, business investment or government expenditures. The GNP available for consumption in a country is reduced by exports, but fortunately, there is a mechanism by which that which is lost can be recouped, namely, imports.

We export goods and services which we have and foreigners want, and import foreign goods and services that we want. It is a mutually beneficial exchange. Imports, then, add to the GNP that is available for our consumption.

The real issue is the net result of our exporting set against our importing. If we export exactly the same value of goods and services as we import, our available GNP is not diminished by our export activity. Our net exports (i.e. exports (X) minus imports (M)), are entered into the national accounts.

In summary then, the GNP consists of four main components: consumption (C), investment (I), government (G) and net exports ($X-M$). In symbols we can write this statement down as:

$$Y = C + I + G + (X-M)$$

In economics, we often use symbols to express in a shortened form statements that we can make in a longer, literary form. There is absolutely no need to panic when you see a statement in symbolic form, providing you look carefully at what the symbols mean, and in this text you will find no statements in symbols that are not fully explained in words.

Chapter 7

Value added

AT ANY ONE MOMENT IN AN ECONOMY there are myriads – literally hundreds of thousands – of inter-connected transactions taking place between two or more parties. Buyers and sellers meet each other to negotiate, haggle and eventually agree to exchange goods for money, or money for goods (or not, as the case may be, if they cannot find mutually acceptable terms for doing business).

In any economy, there are chains of transactions to go through before the goods and services that households consume appear as final goods in the market place. The motor vehicle that is standing gleaming-new in the showroom, starts off as unprocessed raw materials which are transformed into steel, machined into parts and assembled into finished vehicles; the bread we eat, must first be grown as wheat, milled into flour, and baked into bread before it reaches our table; and both these, and the thousands of other products we might wish to consume, require many other goods and services in side-transactions before they can be supplied as finished goods for our consumption. Motor vehicle manufacturers invest in buildings, use land, purchase electricity, paint, parts, and the services of marketing specialists; and the baker requires heat for the ovens, vans to distribute the loaves to shops, and packaging to keep them fresh; while the farmer uses fields, fertilisers, tractors, harvesters, bags, and lorries to get the original wheat to the millers, who, in turn, use buildings, machinery, and electricity to turn wheat into flour.

Now if we were to attempt to add up all these transactions, we would not only have a mammoth task on our hands, it would also be pretty pointless. The double-, treble- and quadruple-counting involved would make the entire statistical exercise of absolutely no use whatsoever. For what would be the meaning of counting up the value of the transactions between farmers and the miller, and then between the miller and the baker, and finally, between the shopkeeper who sells the bread and the consumer?

To settle this point we can use a very simple imaginary arithmetical example, as set out in Table 1(*a*), in which we add each transaction together in an attempt to add up the value of all the transactions that take place to produce bread.

In Table 1(*a*) the farmer sells his wheat crop to the miller for $10, and the miller turns the wheat into flour and sells it to the baker for $20 (being $10 for what he paid the farmer for the wheat and another $10 for

TABLE 1(a): **Value of transactions (bread supply)**

Activity	Output	$ value of transactions
farming	wheat	10
milling	flour	20
baking	bread	30
retailing	distribution	40
Total transactions		100

what it cost him to process the wheat at a profit and transport it to the baker). The baker paid the miller $20 for the flour and after baking the bread, sold his output to the retail shops for $30, which covers his costs of acquiring the flour from the miller, his costs of making bread (again, we assume at a profit) and his transport costs. The retail shopkeepers sell the bread to consumers for $40.

But what is the price of the bread to the consumer? Is it the $40 that the retailers charge, and if it is, what happened to the $100 that is the 'total value' of all the transactions? Clearly, it cannot be the case that something apparently 'costing' $100, ends up being sold for $40, otherwise where did the $60 go? There is obviously something very wrong here with the 'total value of all transactions' at $100 in Table 1(a).

The answer is revealing, and it is, furthermore, very important for your understanding of economics. If we simply add up all economic transactions that occur in a process of producing final goods for consumers we would be 'double counting' each transaction, if we proceed as we have done in Table 1(a).

When the miller buys wheat from the farmer (at $10) and processes it into flour, he must sell the flour at a price that covers what he paid the farmer for the wheat and what it cost him to process it. This latter cost must cover the wages he pays to his employees, the cost of the use of his machinery (known as depreciation), his transport costs, and whatever profit margin he sets for his activity. In Table 1(a), we suggest that his own costs (including profit) comes to $10, and, therefore, the sales revenue he earns from supplying flour must be $20.

Now the baker buys in flour at $20, and you can consider this as being composed of $10 he is paying the miller, who has already paid the farmer for his contribution of wheat, and another $10 he is paying the miller for turning the wheat into flour and delivering it to his premises. But the baker also has costs (wages, depreciation, transport and profit), and these turn out to be $10. Hence, the baker passes on to the retailer what it cost him for the flour he bought from the miller ($20), and his own costs of $10, giving him a target revenue from bread sales of $30.

If he receives anything less than $30 – perhaps retailers do not want to buy much bread that week, or they consider his prices are too high – he will suffer losses and either find a way of producing bread at a price that

42 · Value added

retailers are prepared to pay, or he will have to consider getting out of the baking business.

The retailer sells loaves of bread to households and aims for a sales revenue that will cover his costs of acquiring the loaves from the baker ($30) and also his own costs of operating a retail establishment (in this imaginary example, $10). This means the baker must aim for $40 from the sale of bread to consumers. This is the price of bread for final consumers (what the price is per loaf would depend on how many loaves there were in the consignment from the baker; if there were 100 loaves in the consignment, then each loaf would sell for 40c).

It certainly could not be $100, which is the total from adding each transaction together, rather than from adding what each transactor *adds* to costs of buying output from the previous transactor. Again, let us put this in a simple arithmetical example set out in Table 1(*b*), using the information given in Table 1(*a*).

TABLE 1(*b*): **Value added by each transactor**

Activity	Output	Bought-in costs	Own costs	Sales revenue
farmer	wheat	0	10	10
miller	flour	10	10	20
baker	bread	20	10	30
retailer	distribution	30	10	40
Total 'own costs' value added			40	

The 'own costs' are what each transactor contributes, or *adds*, to the value of the final product, in this case bread sold to consumers. We call this the *value added* by each transactor. You can see from Table 1(*b*) that the value added (shown in the column headed 'own costs') is $40, and this corresponds exactly to the sales revenue of bread to final consumers. For the retailer who receives the $40, he covers his bought-in costs of $30 and his added value of $10.

Nobody loses from this transaction. There is no sleight-of-hand involved from the calculation of value added. The misleading total of the value of all transactions in Table 1(*a*) arises because of the 'double-counting' of each transaction instead of the counting of each transactor's contribution to the value of the final product in the hands of the consumer. The charge to the consumer covers all costs of previous transactions plus the value added by the final transactor.

What happens to the value added? It is divided between the producers of output and constitutes their incomes from economic activity. Employees receive wages, and the owners of businesses (called capitalists) receive profits.

In the example in Table 1(*b*), the retailer pays his employees their wages and keeps for himself his profit. He must take this out of the $40, but only after paying the baker $30 for supplying him with bread. But, right along the chain of production, the value added at each stage is paid to the producers, either as wages for selling labour services or as profit for owning the business.

If we add up the value added by all economic activities within a given time period (usually a year) we will get a measure of the value of all economic activity in that country. In effect, we are measuring the *national income*, for this is what the population has earned from producing national output during that year. There is no double-counting, and the economic meaning of the concept of national income is perfectly clear: it is what society has earned from engaging in economic activity; if the national income this year is greater than it was last year (assuming no changes in prices due to inflation, of which more later!), we know unambiguously that the economy has grown this year compared with last year. In a word, it is *richer*.

If, on the other hand, the national income is smaller this year compared with last year, we know that we are poorer – there is less to go around than there was last year. With a smaller value added it must be that employees have less to spend on consumption because their wages are lower or there are fewer of them employed than there were last year, or the owners of businesses are receiving smaller profits for some reason, and they may be considering getting out of business or reducing the number of employees, or both.

It is the aim of macroeconomic policy to arrange appropriate circumstances for the national income to grow, rather than diminish. People generally prefer to become richer, to have more income available for personal consumption. This means that the economy has to increase its activity to increase the value added, which appears as income to households, and economic policies directed to these ends are described as policies for economic growth.

National income accounts are a means by which we can measure the success, or otherwise, of a country's policies towards economic growth.

Chapter 8

The national income accounts

THE GROSS NATIONAL PRODUCT (GNP) is the most useful aggregate measure of the economic activity of a country. From earlier chapters you now have enough knowledge of economic concepts to put them together to arrive at an understanding of what we mean by the GNP. There are three ways of measuring GNP, though these are really different aspects of the same thing. Our first approach will be to elaborate on the value added measure of GNP, and then show how the other measures (expenditure and output) are really the same thing in a different guise.

National income is another name for the total flow of value added in all economic activities. In the bread example of Chapter 7, we found the value added of that particular production cycle (from farmer's wheat to consumers' bread) to be $40. If we added together all the value added of all the production cycles of all the goods and services in an economy over the period of a year we would arrive at a measure of the national income.

In Table 2, I have put together the national income accounts of the 'Ogoland' economy (a wholly imaginary country that I have used for many years in lectures and books), and by working through the figures you will improve your understanding of what these accounts mean, and why they are constructed in the way they are in Table 2 (which, though referring to an imaginary economy, should be thought of as representative of a real economy, such as yours).

The distinction between market and non-market sectors in an economy is a useful one, which we shall use in later chapters when we look at controversies about what the appropriate balance between private and public sectors should be to generate economic growth.

The distinction has origins as far back as Adam Smith, though he developed the idea of a two-sector economy around the distinction between, what he called, 'productive' and 'unproductive' labour; the former was regarded as labour that reproduced its own value, and the productive capacity used up in production, in contrast with the latter, which merely consumed its value on a 'once-and-for-all' basis. An example of the former would be labourers who produced clothes which were sold at a price that covered their costs of production (wages for labour, depreciation of capital, and profits of enterprise); and an example of the latter would be labourers who provided personal services for their employers (butlers, maids, private secretaries, etc.), for their wages did

TABLE 2: **National income accounts for Ogoland, 1988 ($billion)**

Economic activity (1)	Sales revenue (2)	Bought-in costs (3)	Value added (4)	Employment incomes (5)	Profits (6)
1. *Market sector*					
farming & fishing	3.0	1.3	1.7	0.56	1.14
oil, gas	6.0	2.4	3.6	0.1	3.5
mining	4.0	1.6	2.4	1.79	0.61
manufacturing	46.0	25.9	20.1	18.8	1.3
construction	6.0	2.4	3.6	3.0	0.6
electricity	2.0	0.9	1.1	0.7	0.4
transport & communication	6.0	2.0	4.0	3.5	0.5
distribution	14.0	6.0	8.0	6.2	1.8
other services	13.0	3.5	9.5	5.5	4.0
2. Sub-total	100.0	46.0	54.0	40.15	13.85
3. *Non-market sector*			7.0	7.0	—
4. Total value added (2+3)			61.0	47.15	13.85
5. Inputed rent from dwellings			2.8		2.8
6. *Gross Domestic Product* (GDP) (4+5)			63.8		
7. Net property income from abroad			1.0		1.0
8. *Gross National Product* (GNP) (6+7)			64.8		
9. Depreciation			−4.8	—	−4.8
10. *Net National Income* (8+9)			60.0	47.15	12.85

not reproduce their costs – their employer consumed their services as part of his or her standard of living.

But Smith's distinction is altogether too narrow for a modern economy. Today we distinguish between activities that produce goods and services for sale in markets from goods and services that are distributed on some other basis, such as by governments.

In the market sector, value added is found by deducting the costs of bought-in materials from sales revenue. Once the bought-in costs are met, the remainder, the value added, is available to be distributed between employees as income for their labour services and owners of businesses (the capitalists or shareholders) as profits for their enterprise and risk.

The non-market sector provides us with a minor problem: governments do not supply their goods and services in a market; they purchase them from a market but do not dispose of them in one. There is, therefore, no sales revenue accruing from government activities. People, however, are employed (in their hundreds of thousands!) by governments. They supply labour services in their roles as public administrators, members of the armed and police forces, members of the judiciary, including the prison service, medical and other staff in public hospitals, teachers in state schools, and as personnel in numerous other functions.

Government services are part of the output of an economy, and we assume that government output is valued by society – if somebody pays for something we consider it an economic activity, and it is not for economists to make value judgements as to whether any particular economic activity is more or less worthy than another. If there is a prejudice against certain government activities, this must not cloud our judgement about its economic relevance. If it is paid for, it is valued, and that is the end of the matter.

Our problem is to give a monetary value to government output where its relative value is not tested in a market. We know the value of market output because we know what people are willing to pay for it – simply multiply the amount of market output sold by the price at which it is sold (quantity times price equals monetary value of the output). In the absence of a market for government output, we must rely on the expenditure that society is prepared to make to have government produce that output. Hence, we simply take the wages bill for all government services and add that to the value added from the market sector.

In Table 2, you will find the value added of the market sector as $54 billion (row 2, column 4), to which is added the wages for non-market activity of $7 billion (row 3), to give a total value added for the economy of $61 billion (row 4). This value added is divided between employment incomes ($47.15 billion) and profits ($13.85 billion).

The market sector is shown with nine industries ('Farming' to 'Other services' in column 1), and the sales revenue ($100 billion) that they earned in 1988 is shown in column 2, followed in column 3 by the bought-in costs ($46 billion). When bought-in costs are deducted from sales revenue the value added is found. To avoid double counting, for reasons explained in Chapter 7 (manufacturing, for example, uses electricity), we find the value added in each industry in the market sector (column 4), and this is divided between employment incomes ($40.15 billion) (column 5) and profits ($13.85 billion) (column 6).

There are, of course, no profits in the government non-market sector (what the government provides is not sold to raise a revenue) and government value added consists of its entire employees' wages bill ($7 billion in column 5), which is added to the employment incomes in the market sector ($40.15 billion), to produce total employment income of $47.15 billion (column 5, row 4).

If you look at the share of market value added going to profits ($13.85 billion in column 6), you will see that there are three other entries in this column, and an explanation of their role will introduce you to some new concepts.

First, note the entry 'Imputed rent from dwellings' (row 5). This arises because home ownership provides owners of dwellings with certain benefits, not the least of which is that they do not have to pay rent! Some households do not, however, own the dwellings they live in; they rent them from landlords or public authorities. The proportion of rented dwellings out of the total housing stock varies from country to country. In Scotland, for instance, most dwellings are let to tenants by local governments, while in England the reverse situation applies – most dwellings are owned by those living in them.

If we counted only rented dwellings among economic transactions in the national accounts, we would be in danger of making a nonsense of our carefully measured figures if, for any reason, there was a change in the status of those living in rented accommodation.

Suppose, for example, local governments decided to sell off a proportion of their public housing stock. If public housing was sold to tenants, we would see a drop in national income, caused by nothing more than a shift from tenant to owner-occupier status, because the amount collected in rents would fall. Or, vice versa, if people changed from being home owners to tenants, the national income would increase, because the amount collected in rents would rise. But, when you consider it carefully, you will see that nothing of any meaningful economic significance has occurred – the same amount of housing services exists before and after these changes in ownership and tenant status.

This leaves us with the choice of including some more or less representative estimate of the value to owners of the benefits of owning their properties – an imputed rental value – or suffering a damaging challenge to the credibility of our national income calculations.

Naturally, in the face of potential criticism, economists have chosen to diverge from starkly simple calculations and to require that national income statistics include, under value added and profits, an estimate of the rental value of privately owned property. In Table 2 this estimated value is $2.8 billion. While this is a value added contribution it certainly does not constitute an income of employment (for in what sense are they employing themselves?); it is wholly an income accruing to owners of dwellings, and, therefore, is entered under the profits column for distributed value added.

We must now distinguish between what appear to be synonymous categories. I refer to the distinction between 'domestic' and 'national' income. Domestic economic activity takes place within the actual territory of the country.

Every member country of the United Nations has clearly defined geographic borders (subject to the occasional challenge of neighbours!). Whatever economic activity takes place within these defined geographic borders, is designated as *domestic*.

The sum total of all economic activities within the geographic borders of a country is its Gross *Domestic* Product (GDP). Hence, in Table 2, GDP (row 6) is defined as the total value added of all enterprises in the time period (usually a year), plus the imputed rent for home owners (dwellings are clearly within the domestic territory). In Table 2, GDP is assessed at $63.8 billion.

If you cast your mind back to earlier chapters you will remember that economic activity, (Y), consists of household consumption, plus business investment, plus government expenditure, plus the net balance of foreign trade (exports [X] minus imports [M]). At any one moment, various individuals, who are nationals of the territory, will own, or be owed, sums of money from investments in foreign countries. At the same time, some people, resident abroad, will own shares and other obligations in businesses or government bonds in the domestic territory.

The significance of this is that foreign owners of domestic businesses, and domestic owners of foreign businesses, repatriate, or have sent back to their own countries, their earnings from ownership (profits and dividends).

With some profits being sent back to their owners' countries, and some profits from other countries arriving in the home country, there is a net sum available, which if it is positive (your nationals own more profitable businesses abroad than foreigners own profitable businesses in your country) will add to the flow of domestic value added, and hence your country's well-being. If it is negative – foreigners own more profitable businesses in your country than your nationals own abroad – it will reduce your domestic value added.

In Table 2, the entry in row 7 for 'Net property income from abroad' is worth $1 billion, and this is added to Gross Domestic Product ($63.8 billion) to produce Gross *National* Product ($64.8 billion) (row 8). The Gross National Product (GNP) is *national* because it represents what the nationals of your country earn as value added, irrespective of where in the world – domestic or abroad – that they earn it. Because net property income is a *net* sum, we have deducted the earnings of foreign nationals from our domestic product, and everything that remains represents the earnings of our nationals alone.

If we live in a country with an economy that is heavily penetrated by foreign nationals as investors and producers, the net flow of value added outwards is likely to reduce our domestic product below what it would be if all our domestic activities were owned by our own nationals, or if our nationals owned more businesses abroad.

Now this is a contentious issue, though many politicians make a crude mistake when contemplating a national economy with a negative statistic for net property income from abroad. They see a flow of property income going abroad and develop covetous economic policies to try to reverse it. In the absence of foreign development of national resources, it may be that there would be no, or a much slower, development of them, and it is often the case that sudden, perhaps violent, reversals of policy that drive out foreign investors, do so much damage to a development programme that instead of having a slightly smaller GDP from repatriated profits, the country ends up with a much reduced GDP as foreign investment and confidence is destroyed.

A judgement is required, that balances dissatisfaction with a negative flow of repatriated profits with the benefits to the domestic economy of value added, particularly from employment of nationals, that is created by foreign investment. The value added that is created is, in many cases, much greater than the value added that is repatriated.

Finally, in Table 2, we have an entry for 'Depreciation' (row 9), which is the estimated sum of capital equipment, etc. that is used up in the course of producing the year's output. This is the cost of creating output; it is no longer available as capacity to create new output and it must therefore be replaced. By diverting some of this year's output into replacing last year's used up capital, we must show this in our national income accounts as a debit to be taken away from the GNP ($64.8 billion in row 8). In fact, GNP minus depreciation is Net National Income (row 10); in Ogoland's case it is:

$$\$64.8 - 4.8 = \$60 \text{ billion}.$$

In our simple example, earnings from employment will be spent by households on consumption goods and services, and earnings in the form of profits will be spent by businesses on investment goods (purchased, of course, from other businesses). Taken at its simplest (that is, ignoring the complication of household savings and what happens to them), we can say that the total expenditure of households on consumption and the total expenditure of businesses on investment will be equal to the value added in the year.

At the same time, and by a similar logic, we could add up the total value of consumption output from businesses, and add that to the total value of investment output from businesses, and find the value of final output, which must be exactly equal to the amount spent by households and businesses on final output and also equal to the amount they earn from employment and ownership.

In other words, we can calculate the GNP by any of three methods that

50 · The national income accounts

measure the monetary value of: income, expenditure and output in the economy. The logical connection ought to be obvious: if what is earned is spent, the two totals must be the same, and by extension, if what is earned is spent on output, it must follow that the value of output must equal what it costs to purchase it, and this is turn must equal the amount of income available for purchasing output.

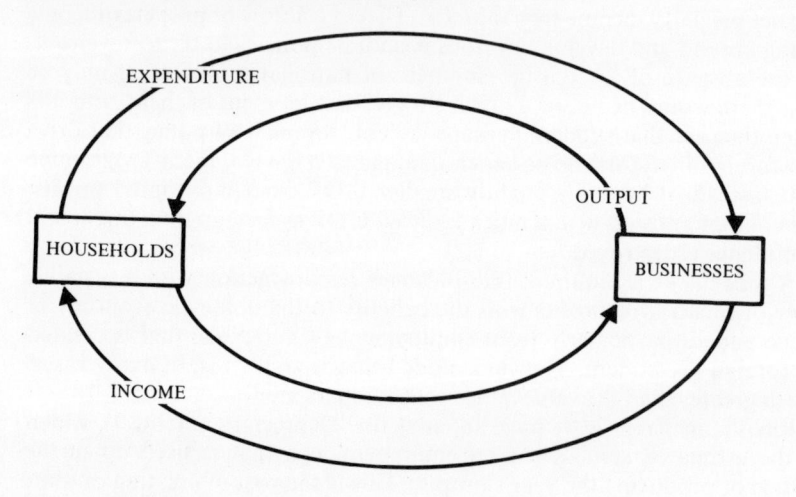

FIG. 4: The circular flow of income between households and businesses

In short, the three totals of income, expenditure and output are the same thing measured from different points in the circular flow of income between households and businesses. This is illustrated in Fig. 4, where, for simplicity, I have not shown investment transactions between businesses, but confined the model to a GNP consisting of: household labour services; value added from employment; and household purchases of final consumption goods and services. This does not alter the general principle at all: GNP can be measured by any of the three methods, and in the real world this is precisely what happens.

National statistical offices calculate GNP by each method and compare the results, and generally they are fairly close, though a small discrepancy is inevitable (if only because of the diverse sources for statistical data) and the totals are adjusted by use of a 'residual' addition or subtraction, usually a number under one per cent of the total.

Chapter 9

GNP critically examined

THAT ECONOMICS, AS A SUBJECT, is not a settled body of doctrine, ought very quickly to become obvious to you, and nowhere is this more true than in the relatively straightforward area of national income accounting. The fact that large amounts of GNP data have been collected for practically every country in the world, in some countries with greater accuracy and credibility than others, does not amount to evidence that controversies about the concept of the GNP are settled and that the work on GNP statistics is now simply a routine activity devoid of and kind of dissension or debate.

If the debate has abated recently this has more to do with the controversies remaining unsettled and the debaters feeling jaded, rather than with anything being resolved, and it is appropriate, even in an introductory text, that your attention is drawn to some of these issues, just in case you get a wholly unrepresentative picture of macroeconomics, for, if there is one thing worse than believing that economics has nothing to contribute to human welfare, it is the belief that nothing else besides economics can do so.

The main confusion among those who criticise conventional measures of GNP (you can see I do not intend to remain neutral in these debates!) is to overstate the importance that economists place on the GNP as a measure of human 'happiness' or welfare.

GNP measures economic activity not human happiness; to say that the GNP has risen in one year compared with another, is to say absolutely nothing about whether the people are better or worse off as a result. As yet there is no known measurement of human happiness, and all attempts so far to find one have caused much dissension, particularly among those who believe we *ought* to have such a measure. The only thing that unites those who believe that human happiness is, or ought to be, measurable, is a rejection by all of them of GNP as such a measure.

People who criticise GNP calculations certainly have an implicit belief that human happiness is measurable, for they invariably assert that people are worse off now than they were before, and to make this assertion it is necessary to believe that we can compare one state of society with another. But, from a scientific point of view, it is not possible to make an objective judgement as to whether people are 'better off' either than they were in the past, or than they might have been if things had been arranged differently. All such assertions are the value-judgements of those who make them.

Nevertheless, criticism of GNP measures has persisted, and while much of this criticism is misdirected, often consisting of a strawman set up for an easy knockdown, some of it highlights aspects of national income accounting, which otherwise might remain hidden, and also allows us to focus on some policy issues which otherwise might not be raised.

Human welfare is something much greater than economic welfare. In fact, economic welfare is a relatively narrow concept that tries to cope with those aspects of human welfare that can be related to 'the measuring rod of money', and clearly many aspects of human welfare cannot be measured in money terms at all. (If you doubt this, how much is the innocent, happy laughter of children worth in cash?)

If aspects of human welfare cannot be brought within the ambit of money, as surely applies, say, in a parent's love of his or her child, or in the feeling of pride in personal achievement, then economic measures of welfare have nothing – absolutely nothing – to say (directly) about them. The cost of the food that parents buy to feed their children can be measured; how tenderly, or otherwise, they prepare the food for their children cannot be measured. The distinction has been clear to economists since Professor A. C. Pigou, of Cambridge University in England, first stated it more than sixty years ago in *The Economics of Welfare* (1920). That some critics (including some economists, who should have known better) have set about attacking the concept of the GNP, on the spurious grounds that economists are not aware of the distinction, is, in a scholarly sense, wholly discreditable.

National income accounting measures that portion of human welfare that can be measured by direct or indirect monetary transactions. The fact that economic activity (or the lack of it) has a major role in human welfare, including happiness, is fairly obvious. How much, and to what extent, economic activity contributes to human welfare and happiness is, quite properly, an impossible question to answer – each of us can differ in the weight we accord to monetary transactions in the sum total of our happiness (or anybody else's). But to assert, broadly, that those persons in abject poverty, deprived of resources and without hope of acquiring any, are unlikely to be as happy as they could be, if their needs were met, is hardly a challengeable proposition.

It might be more challengeable if we were to assert, which we do not, that relatively affluent persons are *necessarily* happier than persons whose basic needs are not being met; but here, the strength of the challenge would turn on how much weight we placed on the word 'necessarily'. Affluent people may or may not be happier than those whose basic needs are not being matched by available resources. There is no way of knowing who is happier, or who is more miserable. The GNP statistic does not tell us, and was never meant to do so. To assert that it does is a nonsense.

Arguments along this line generally take the following form: when a steel plant produces steel, the GNP goes up by what it costs in value added per ton; but steel plants also produce smoke and slag waste, which pollute the environment, and no account is taken of this disagreeable consequence in the GNP. To find the 'true' GNP, therefore, we should deduct from the 'crude' GNP the consequential environmental damage created by the steel plant.

Problems, of course, abound in even considering this suggestion. For instance: how much should we deduct from the GNP to cover the losses in welfare caused by pollution? If pollution is simply dumped into the local environment, there is no question that human welfare is lower as a result. People living near to the steel works will have smoke wafting across their homes, probably dirtying their washing, and, at least, making it less pleasant to go about their private business. Also, heaps of slag waste littered around the area are by and large unattractive backdrops to live beside.

In the absence of agreement on how much to deduct from ordinary GNP to produce a welfare-related GNP, we are left to make our own value judgements. If, however, the steel plant is compelled to take counter-measures against its pollution, which means, essentially, spending money on anti-pollution activities, we have a ready-made measure of how much the community values a pollution-free environment by answering the question: how much does it spend on reducing pollution activities?

Whereas the proposition, that GNP should include the negative value of the consequential damage to the environment, starts out requiring the GNP statistic to be reduced by some allowance for environmental damage, when we find a means of measuring what the damage is worth to the community – by how much it spends to prevent or reduce it – we are led not to a reduction in GNP, but to its increase.

We must, in fact, add the costs of anti-pollution activities to the GNP if they are undertaken by the community. This follows, logically, even from the critics' point of view: if untreated environmental damage is to be taken away from the GNP (assuming we could value it, which I have suggested we cannot), it follows that the treatment of pollution must be added to the GNP. Far from the pollution criticism being a fundamental blow at the concept of monetary GNP measures, it is, in fact, an endorsement of them.

A similar reasoning would apply to other disamenities that are allegedly associated with rising GNP, for example, urban squalor, social stress, mass tourism, noise, lower standards of law and order, drug addiction, crimes of violence, break-up of families and so on. Whether any or all of these alleged consequences are solely attributable to a rising GNP is disputable, but the point remains, that trying to value them in a monetary sense for purposes of transforming the GNP into a measure of general welfare is at best futile and at worse a gross misunderstanding of what is involved in the measurement of GNP. Only those actual *expenditures* directed towards tackling these problems can properly be picked up in GNP measures, because the GNP measures humankind's economic activities and not human happiness.

Moreover, as we have no way of knowing, if no growth took place, whether these disagreeable disamenities would be on a lesser scale, or replaced by other disamenities of a worse character (mass starvation, disease, civil violence, mass ignorance, tyranny and so on) we cannot in all honesty press for a policy of reversing economic growth as measured by the GNP.

One thing we might consider, however, is that people the world over, when given the choice of remaining at a very low economic level, with a small GNP per capita, or of rising towards a higher economic level, with a higher GNP per capita, appear to prefer, on the whole and on average (there are always exceptions!) the latter. Indeed, observation suggests that human migration is mainly, if not exclusively, from poorer to richer societies, and while this in itself can contribute to serious social problems (overcrowding, urban squalor, exploitation of, and violent antagonism towards, immigrants, etc.), it does not support the view that the burdens of economic growth, as measured by GNP statistics, are of such overwhelming significance that people choose to avoid growth economies in favour of stagnant or primitive ones.

Some economists have remained firmly convinced that standard GNP statistics are not satisfactory and have advocated changes along the lines discussed above, with one or two refinements of a more positive nature. Two such distinguished American economists are William Nordhaus and James Tobin ('Is Growth Obsolete?', National Bureau of Economic Research, *Fiftieth Anniversary Colloquium*, Columbia University Press, 1972). They proposed a new measure to replace GNP, which they called 'Measureable Economic Welfare' (MEW). This measure included allowances for items normally excluded from GNP, such as the improved opportunities for leisure activities in a richer economy compared with a poorer one, and the domestic services of home-based parents (usually women) and other 'non-market' activities.

Against the plus items, presently excluded from the GNP (because of real difficulties in placing a monetary value on non-monetary transactions), Nordhaus and Tobin argued for deductions for what they termed 'regrettable necessities'. In this category, they included defence, police, sanitation, and the costs of urbanisation.

The net effect of their calculations that adjusted United States GNP statistics for earlier years, by taking account of estimates of the pluses (e.g. increased and improved leisure opportunities) and minuses (e.g. pollution, and 'regrettable necessities'), was to produce MEW totals for each year that were different from conventionally measured GNP totals. But the trend figures for MEW statistics of United States economic activities during 1929 to 1965 were still upwards, albeit that they showed a slower rate of annual growth than those measures which were based on conventional GNP.

In my view, the adjusted measures of GNP (MEW, etc.) are brave, though futile, attempts to improve a carefully constructed measure by grafting on more or less immeasurable, though none the less real, attributes of a modern economy.

Deducting defence expenditures from the GNP, for example, on the ground that defence is not purchased for its own sake, and is not therefore a contribution to household welfare, even though defence is normally a prudent provision against the very real risks of invasion and war, opens up a conceptual minefield. If there was no risk of war – all territories everywhere were inviolate from the depredations of neighbours – there would be no need for defence expenditures. The risks of war, however, are very real, as current and recent wars indicate. The opportunity cost of defence provision in foregone civilian programmes may be high, but the opportunity cost of no defence at all could very well be much higher.

Defence is a necessary expenditure, as Nordhaus and Tobin agree, but whether it is regrettable is not really relevant. Defence consumes economic resources, and the GNP measures this consumption in exactly the same way that it measures health expenditures (which would not be necessary if there was no illness), education expenditures (necessary because we are not born with all the knowledge we need), food expenditures (needed only because we eat to survive) and so on, through practically everything we consume.

To argue that there must be a distinction between necessities that are regrettable and those that are not, would lead us to an incredible confusion, and for no great purpose.

For instance, do we separate food and drink consumption that keeps us barely alive from the excess consumption that titillates our palates? The former is, presumably, a regrettable necessity, and therefore deducted from MEW, and the latter unnecessary, and, in view of the problems of obesity etc. surely also regrettable, and therefore ought to be deducted too!

If, on the other hand, basic food requirements are necessary and *not* regrettable, even though it is only hunger and thirst that forces us to consume them, what is the logical distinction between food in this role and defence as a counter to the risks of war, or, for that matter, between fire services as a counter to the risk of fire, clothing as a counter to the facts of climate, unused but prudently carried umbrellas as a counter to the risk of rain, serum as a counter to the risks of snake-bite, and in fact, everything we can think of outside of a Garden of Eden where all is provided, all is comfort, and not a tear is shed in want, fear or regret?

That there are problems associated with the conventional measure of GNP must be conceded, but the solutions that have been adopted to meet these problems are probably as consistent with practical needs as we can get, though, as with much in economics, there is always scope for improvement if something can be suggested that does not make the anomalies in the GNP calculation worse, or more numerous.

Take depreciation for example. We deduct depreciation from Gross National Product, to produce a figure for Net National Product, in order to recognise the fact that capital is used up in the course of production and has to be replaced if the economy is to keep the same capacity to produce in year 2 as it had in year 1.

Depreciation is a notoriously slippery quantity. Businesses, typically, relate their announced depreciation charges more to the needs of their tax obligations than to the neatness or accuracy of GNP measures. Businesses depreciate a machine according to a current applicable tax formula which may or may not bear any resemblance to the actual lifetime use of the machine.

If, for instance, the tax authorities permit depreciation in the first year of purchase, the entire cost of the machine is set against that year's profits, and, consequently, the business owes the government less profits tax than it would if the depreciation were restricted to, say, one twentieth of the cost per year over twenty years. The incentive effect of full depreciation in the first year would encourage businesses to purchase capital goods, and thereby, hopefully increase economic growth in future years, which presumably is the government's intention.

This does not help the accuracy of the adjusted GNP figures, and, as it is patently impossible for the GNP statisticians to make an individual judgement on the actual depreciation of the capital stock of every individual business in the economy, the depreciation figures must be more than a trifle arbitrary.

The replacement figures for an economy's capital stock are made less reliable by the fact of technological progress. A new dumper truck for a construction site, for example, might embody the latest technical features (power steering, airbrakes, longer-life tyres, more powerful transmission, anti-roll bars, powerful night lights, etc.) which were not present in the truck it replaces. Some portion, but how much is not easy to judge, of the replacement expenditure is actually enhancing the productive capacity of the trunk, and it is not therefore strictly exclusively a replacement expenditure at all. With technological enhancement we have a quality improvement in the capacity of the capital stock over time, which is not easy to include in net investment.

Rising costs, some part of which are caused by price inflation and some part by quality enhancement, understate the depreciation total in the GNP. Accountants allow for depreciation against the original ('historic') cost of the equipment and not the replacement cost which will be faced in the future. By understating depreciation in this way, net investment is overstated. The probability of an overstatement in net investment, from the use of historic and not replacement costs, being exactly matched by an overstatement in depreciation from embodied technical progress, remains an empirical question for GNP statisticians, and any adjustments they make to the figures, even on well founded assumptions, must still have an element of arbitrariness about them.

I have mentioned already the problem of non-marketed services in respect of the government sector, and why these expenditures are counted at their employment cost in value added calculations. There are other non-marketed costs which are not open to this kind of treatment, and for this reason are excluded from the GNP accounts.

I refer to the labour services of parents in their households. These services, as any parent will testify, are no small burden. Washing, cleaning, cooking, repairing, entertaining, child-minding, chauffeur-driving children to school, parties, boy scouts/girl guides, and driving others to stations, shops, restaurants, and theatres, gardening, painting, general household repairs and so on, can, and regularly do, take up much time and energy in any household. Where these services are carried out without monetary reward, though they involve real effort, they are not included in the GNP.

Where a household employs servants, or tradespeople, including taxi drivers, etc., to supply labour services for a monetary charge, these charges appear in the GNP. This leads to the well known student's favourite GNP-anomaly of the case where a man marries his housekeeper. Formerly he paid her wages and these were part of the GNP; after the marriage, he no longer pays her wages and the GNP is reduced by that amount! (Fortunately, for statistical purposes, the cases of men marrying their housekeepers, or women marrying their gardeners, are rare!)

Household labour services for family purposes are not included in the GNP because of the practical difficulties of counting them, and not because these services are regarded as of no consequence. Parental services are extremely important to a household (as father and children find out if mother is in hospital!).

Similarly, those labour services involved in Do-It-Yourself activities, such as home maintenance of the motor car, D-I-Y home painting, plumbing, repairing, etc., are not counted in GNP, though the supply of D-I-Y materials and tools is counted because these are bought from businesses and involve monetary transactions by the D-I-Y householder.

We have the same problem here as we had with the attribution of the damage done by pollution to the environment. Agreeing on the value of any non-market activity that does not involve a monetary transaction is no easy task for statisticians. To date, nobody has found a solution to this problem – or, nobody has found one that national statistical offices can agree upon – and by convention these activities are excluded from GNP calculations.

The services of living accommodation are imputed and entered into the GNP because rented tenancy is a major item in most countries' expenditures, whereas paid household servants are not. It is easier to impute a value to services flowing from home ownership because of the active market in houses of all types. Coping with the varying contributory services supplied by members of a family in one household compared with another present statistical problems of unimaginable complexity – I know of families where grown children do not clean their own shoes, whereas mine do, for instance.

Lastly, we have the problem that GNP is measured in money, but money does not remain at a constant value one year compared with another. It is as if Professor Pigou's 'measuring rod' is changing shape between each measurement.

GNP measured in 1995 is going to be different from GNP measured in 1985. This is a fairly safe assumption, given the history of price inflation since the 1930s. What this means in practice is that the purchasing power of your national currency will fall throughout the years to 1995 – if you can buy a basket of food for the weekend at $50 today, you can rest assured that you will need more than $50 to buy that same basket of food in 1995. Of course, I can be less sure about just how many more dollars (or whatever the amount will be in your national currency) you will need, because that depends on the future rate of inflation, but I am certain that you will need more.

To get the real, as opposed to the nominal, or monetary, GNP we have to adjust current GNP to take account of price inflation, and we do this by taking a stated year as the base year, and computing all prices of future GNP in terms of the prices prevailing in that year. In effect, we ask: if we bought the same basket of goods today as we bought in the base year, what is their current cost? If it costs 50 per cent more today than in the base year for the same basket of goods, we adjust our monetary GNP downwards to arrive at the real GNP. (By how much we reduce monetary GNP will depend on some fairly complex statistical issues – for instance, is the basket of goods exactly the same?; did all prices rise at the same rate?)

This inflation problem is compounded when we attempt to compare one country's GNP with another's, especially in a time series. The nominal exchange rates of each country's currency may not be a true reflection of the actual economic trends within each country. We shall see in Part IV how foreign currency exchange rates are not always determined by the economic performance of a country, and may in fact reflect (short-term) political choices of their respective governments. This can lead to erroneous comparative GNP statistics.

With these caveats, we can reasonably conclude that though the GNP has several deficiencies, some more or less important than others, and though it has several critics, some more or less credible than others, it remains on the whole a fairly accurate measure of the monetary transactions in an economy. Its anomalies are well understood by statisticians, if not always by people who use GNP statistics for political purposes, and while improvement in conceptual terms is always welcome, as are improvements in collection, processing and interpretation of GNP data, the GNP is a very valuable input to policy-making discussions at national level.

GNP statistics are drawn up to help public bodies formulate their economic policies. They provide information for democratic political opposition to current or proposed economic policies. They provide the inter-face between which economic theories and practical policies can be debated, and the success or failure of past policies can be measured. This alone justifies studying national income accounting.

Chapter 10 — PART II

The Keynesian legacy

IN THE INTERVENING 160 YEARS between publication of the *Wealth of Nations*, by Adam Smith in 1776, and *The General Theory of Employment, Interest and Money*, by John Maynard Keynes in 1936, there was not a lot of controversy about what made a capitalist free market economy work. This was the 'classical' golden age of economics, where a few dozen individuals could, and did, dominate the subject, and they left their mark upon its overall development as 'all rounders' rather than as specialists. Today, the world's annual output of university and college-trained economists runs into many thousands; the days of the 'all rounders' have gone.

The publication of *The General Theory* (usually known thus by its short title) was not on its own responsible for a new era in economics, for it was really a part, albeit a very important part, of a whole series of developments of quite stunning intellectual fervour in the discipline. One economist looking back on the decades around *The General Theory* referred to them, with great insight, as the 'years of high theory'. The developments in economic theory, in combination with many structural changes in the economies of the industrialised nations, especially in the interventionary role of governments, constitute what for many years was regarded as a 'revolution' in economic thinking and practice.

Ironically, the 'Keynesian revolution' in theory, once so confidently expected to have resolved everything left to resolve in the management of an economy, has recently been eclipsed, both by events and by doubts, and while by no means discredited, and certainly by no means buried, it cannot be said to be in half so confident a state as it was ten years ago.

If not dead, and not yet even dying, the Keynesian revolution is certainly over. Intellectually, economists live in a kind of interregnum, still deeply imbued with the theoretical apparatus that *The General Theory* introduced into the textbooks (and the classrooms), and not yet convinced by whatever is going to replace the Keynesian certainties of the years between 1936 and mid-1970s.

This creates a serious problem for today's students of economics, especially students of macroeconomics. They can either learn the techniques and tools of the recent past, or they can learn a whole battery of competing ideas about what was wrong with the policies and theories of the past, without really having much confidence in the credibility of what is offered in its place.

A few years is too short a time to test the full policy implications of alternative programmes of economic management, though in terms of unemployment, low economic growth, and social tensions, the alternatives cannot yet be said to have established themselves as an improvement on what became known, more than a little unfairly to Keynes, as 'Keynesian' economics. His name is often invoked in support of this or that policy, when close study of his life's work suggests he would have taken an entirely different view. This phenomenon can be exasperating when engaged in closely argued debate, because it starts off all kinds of time-wasting side-debates about the 'true' Keynesian view.

For better or worse, the 'Keynesian' apparatus of analysis and prescription constitutes a large part of mainstream economic thinking and teaching. It is necessary, in my view, therefore, to introduce some of it into a post-Keynesian text on macroeconomics. This necessarily means re-running through some debates between Keynes and his predecessors in the knowledge that subsequent events undid some of his criticism, and, also, that current economic problems – unemployment plus inflation – do not lend themselves to a conventional 'Keynesian' solution.

In addition, it is necessary to re-state some classical economic ideas, as they have been re-introduced into the debate, in the context not of a historical survey of the past, but of the current economic management of several major economies.

Students of macroeconomics are, therefore, thrown in at the deep end of controversy, even in an elementary discussion about how we think an economy operates. Our choice of tools of analysis, even before we have begun to get to grips with the subject itself, can immediately identify us on one or other side of the current debate among macroeconomists.

This could be a burden, if we were to let it intimidate us into taking sides before we appreciate the full argument. Fortunately, we can steer clear of these and other pitfalls by approaching our studies with an open mind, determined only to *understand* the issues and not to take sides.

In what follows, we shall work our way through the conventional 'Keynesian' apparatus for analysing what determines the level of income in an economy, taking in the consumption function, the investment multiplier, savings, the marginal propensity to consume, wage stickiness, and fiscal measures to counter unemployment. This is the 'Keynesian legacy', and, like all legacies, while it is disappointing in parts we are still grateful for having one.

After this, we shall look at the 'monetarist' criticism of Keynes, the classical quantity theory of money, the natural unemployment rate, and the remedial policies monetarists promote for countering inflation.

Our purpose remains to elucidate issues rather than to promote a particular policy view. If you wish to apply this or that idea to particular problems you perceive as being relevant to your country, you may, of course, do so, and if you thus become better equipped to make judgements in respect of policy matters this approach will have served its purpose.

Chapter 11

How much economic activity?

EVERYBODY IN ANY ECONOMY CONSUMES, otherwise they would surely perish, but not everybody produces. Biology, let alone social convention, prevents the very young and the very old from being economically active, though how young or how old a person must be to avoid economically active work is a matter of convention. Young children can watch flocks, older people can watch children. If in a household these arrangements release economically active people to go about their activities, it makes sense for such arrangements to become accepted practice.

In urban industrialised societies, legal restrictions on child labour, and officially recognised retirement ages are in force; the boundaries between economically active and economically inactive are more clearly defined. It is not expected that sick people, or people who are emotionally or mentally disturbed, should have to be economically active.

In free societies, people may also choose to be economically inactive, either because they have an alternative source of income (they might have inherited, or won, a fortune), or because of their private household arrangements (one member is economically active and the other does the household chores).

In Fig. 5(*a*), the population of a country is divided up into categories according to whether they are economically active or not, and then into categories depending upon source of income. The economically active draw income from the market or non-market sector if they are employed. The market sector refers to all those activities where the goods and services that they produce are sold in markets, and the non-market sector refers to activities where the output is paid for by taxation or government borrowing. Some people are included in the economically active category if they are temporarily unemployed but are actively seeking work. In Fig. 5(*a*) the unemployed are shown between the employed sectors, as, presumably, they are available for work in either category.

The economically inactive category can vary as a proportion of the total population, but we would expect it to be around fifty per cent of the population in a developed economy. In this category there are two sources of income: either from other members of the household who are economically active, or from past savings and other entitlements, or from the various government-managed schemes for retirement pensions, sick pay, unemployment assurance, etc.

How much economic activity? · 63

```
                         TOTAL POPULATION
                        /                \
          economically active          economically inactive
           /        \                   /              \
   market      non-market      supported by      supported by
 employment    employment      household         transfers
                                earnings         from state
        unemployed
   agriculture    government     children         retired
   oil           local           house parents    sick
   mining        authorities                      unemployable
   manufacturing armed forces                     prisoners
   electricity
   services
   self-employed
```

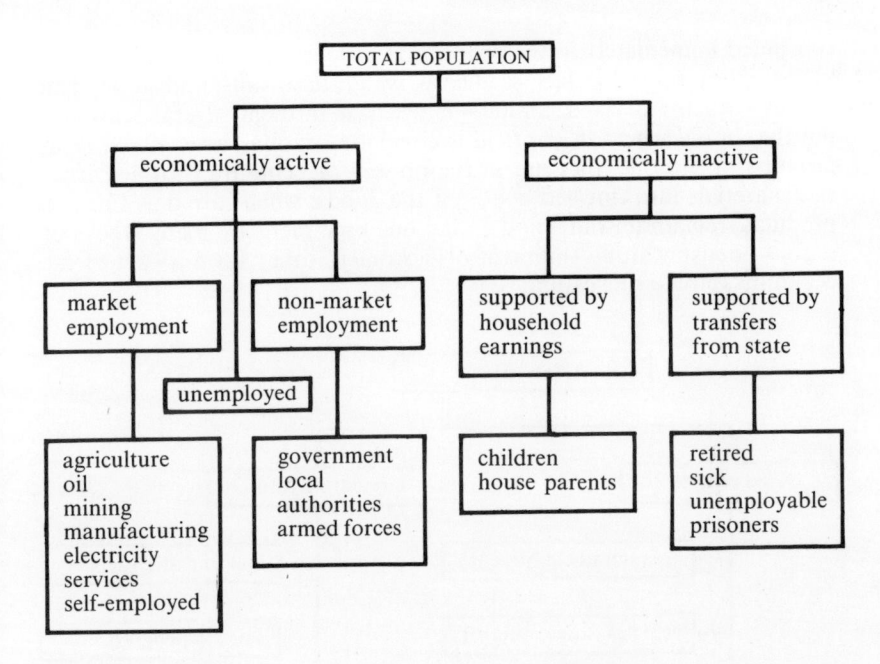

FIG. 5(a): Population – economically active and inactive sections

The exact distribution of a population between the categories will be different in each country, and will probably reflect the level of economic development. You can use Fig. 5(a) to get a detailed statistical description of your own country by entering figures according to your national population statistics.

Labour services are applied to capital to produce output, and the capital stock of an economy at any one time is an important determinant of the level of economic activity. A country with a little, rather than a lot of, capital is likely to be poorer than a country with a lot of, rather than a little, capital. Fig. 5(b) (see page 64) shows the categories into which capital stock can be divided.

The main distinction that is made between categories of capital stock is that between *fixed* and *circulating* capital. The former is usually a much greater proportion of the capital stock than the latter. The distinction is, however, important.

Fixed capital is composed of all those items that are used up over a long time period. Typical examples are: the plant, equipment and machinery of a business; the factories, offices, warehouses, hotels; the road, rail and sewage systems; the stock of business (not household) transport, such as trucks, cars, ships and aircraft; and all houses, apartments and dwellings of households.

Circulating capital is, on the other hand, all those items that are consumed immediately in the production process, such as electricity and fuel supplies, raw materials, seed corn, water, lubricants, and so on. The farmer's tractor is fixed capital – it will last through several seasons – but the unsold wheat in the field is circulating capital, as is all 'work in progress', i.e. inputs that are in the process of being transformed from raw materials into finished goods. If the goods, when stored as finished products, remain unsold – and at any one time there are many stocks of unsold goods awaiting shipment or customers – they form a part of the economy's circulating capital.

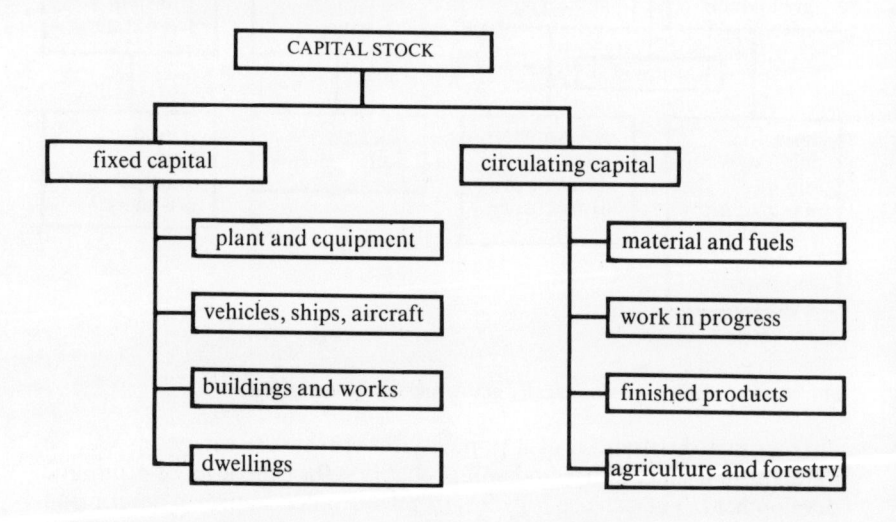

```
                    CAPITAL STOCK
                    /           \
              fixed capital   circulating capital
              - plant and equipment    - material and fuels
              - vehicles, ships, aircraft    - work in progress
              - buildings and works    - finished products
              - dwellings    - agriculture and forestry
```

FIG. 5(b): **Capital stock**

The economically active population and the capital stock of a country constitute the economic potential of an economy. In theory, if the entire economically active population is fully employed and there is no unutilised capital stock, and assuming everybody and everything was being employed in their most efficient roles, the output that could be produced in these circumstances would be at a maximum possible for that economy. This maximum output is known as the *full employment output*.

In the real world, economies seldom, if ever, operate at full capacity. There are unutilised resources present. Some employees, for instance, are in between jobs, perhaps searching for a post more suitable than the ones they had held previously, and are not contributing to output at all. Others are working in industries that have declining demands for their products (perhaps changes in taste are taking place and their employers have not yet adjusted employment levels to the new lower levels of demand) and their retention in less productive employment than might be available elsewhere reduces output below its full potential. Some new people, such as school leavers, recently arrived immigrants from abroad or from other parts of the country, housewives wanting paid work after rearing children, etc., are looking for jobs for the first time.

The phenomenon of unemployed resources caused by temporary dislocations and necessary adjustments to match supply and demand, is called *frictional unemployment*, and it is a necessary experience of a thriving, free market. It means that an economy is always likely to be working below its full potential capacity.

It has long been a central policy of most governments in the industrialised economies to achieve as high a utilisation of economic capacity as is possible, and much of macroeconomic theory is about developing policies that can assist an economy to bring about that desirable result.

This desire for the maximum possible capacity utilisation of labour and the capital stock is made all the more important when the actual utilisation falls well below that engendered by frictional unemployment. If more people are out of work than can possibly be justified by the margin available in an economy to account for frictional unemployment, we have what is known as *structural unemployment*, or unemployment caused by a failure of the economy to bring about needed adjustments in the allocation of labour between expanding and declining industries, or between regions with surplus labour and regions with deficits, or perhaps a general failure to achieve a level of economic activity that could employ all the available resources, even allowing for quite large amounts of frictional unemployment.

The adjustment mechanism may have failed because employees are insisting on wage rates that cannot be justified by the ability of the business to sell the output they produce at prices that cover the costs of employing them. Trade unions, minimum wages legislation, and laws regarding employment, can inhibit the freely functioning price mechanism. Surpluses of labour cannot be eliminated by a cut in everybody's wages; instead, employers cut the numbers employed at the current 'fixed' wage.

It may be that social legislation that transfers incomes from the employed to the unemployed slows down the reaction of a person to the disagreeable effects of unemployment. Instead of a more vigorous search for work, and an acceptance of any job at any wage, the unemployed person sustains a longer search for work, with illusions of greater worth to a potential employer than the real facts suggest should be the case. This prolongs his period of unemployment, until brute facts, including the threat of abject poverty, alter his perception of his likelihood of getting the kind of work he prefers for the wages he thinks he deserves.

The introduction of unemployment benefits to ease the personal burden of unemployment can have the unintended consequence of sustaining relatively higher levels of unemployment than would be the case if unemployment compensation transfers were reduced. But this presents legislators with a real dilemma: the benefits are intended to help those in need of them, and it makes for an unacceptable callousness (at least in democracies) if at the time they really need the benefits they are denied them!

The view that unemployment, beyond levels explained by frictional unemployment, was the result of imperfections in the labour market, caused by trade union and government interference in the workings of the price system and by sociological or cultural factors that had nothing to do with economics, began to be treated with scepticism in the late 1920s. As the depression dragged on through the 1930s, becoming deeper and more depressing, without sign or sight of relief, in Britain, Germany and the United States of America, the sceptics grew more numerous.

It was not that there was a sudden rejection of classical doctrines on unemployment, for many of the sceptics remained firmly within the mainstream of economics and were certainly still very much influenced by its principles and teachings (much as many present day economists remain influenced by what they learned within the 'Keynesian' tradition, this author included!).

Keynes, and those around him at Cambridge University, took the view that whatever validity there was in classical economic theory, it did not fully account for the prolonged depression, and to the extent that it accounted for depression by blaming non-economic forces that 'interfered with the price mechanism', it was totally inadequate as a guide to policy.

If an alternative policy needed to be found and theoretically explained, economists should search for one, otherwise, faced with the world's most serious economic problem, that of massive, sustained and unrelieved unemployment, the economics profession would be in the dubious position of having absolutely nothing to say about it, or worse, having things to say about it that were patently of no operational use because they were directly contrary to the facts.

It is somewhat of a caricature to assert that classical economists believed, and preached, that prolonged unemployment was *impossible*, or, if it was possible, that it had nothing to do with economics, but as is often the case in the real world, the brute course of events seemed to be in conflict with the theories ascribed to classical economics teaching, and, as economists began to have doubts about the classical teachings, they came to believe in the caricature because they desired to do something about the problem of unemployment.

It was into this atmosphere of doubt about the classical teachings (or what people came to believe were classical teachings) that Keynes began to articulate alternative policies (in the 1929 British General Election for the Liberal Party) and then went on to provide by 1936 a theoretical underpinning of the policies he advocated to relieve unemployment. It is to his theoretical apparatus that we shall now turn.

Chapter 12

Effective demand and economic activity

IN NO FIELD OF HUMAN ENDEAVOUR OTHER THAN ECONOMICS is it more true that the intentions of well meaning individuals can be so often frustrated by events. That great Scottish poet, Robert Burns, could have been writing in celebration of the basic economic problem, when he wrote his poem about the nest of field mice being disturbed by the farmer's plough: 'the best laid schemes of mice and men often go astray, and bring sorrow and pain where they promised joy' (an inadequate English translation of the Scots' language!).

What we plan is so often different from what we experience, and this is very evident in economic activity. A great deal that is obscure in economics is often a confusion between what was intended and what actually happened. If you can grasp that distinction, then a lot of economic controversy becomes a great deal easier to follow.

In the circular flow models of Part I, we saw how the incomes that households earned from selling labour services to businesses were spent on the output supplied by those businesses. There was no other place for the output to go to, and nothing else on which to spend household income. As long as this relationship remained the rule, there was neither an excess supply of output, leading to a curtailment by businesses of their desired demand for inputs, nor a deficit demand for goods and services, leading to a reduction in the supply of outputs. If the equilibrium situation between households and businesses changed for any reason, adjustments would have to be made either in the demand for labour services or in the supply of output, or both.

Whatever the level of activity in the simple economy of the circular flow diagram, it is possible for households and businesses to achieve an equilibrium where incomes from employment match incomes from selling output to households. In consequence, you should note that this relationship does not imply that the equilibrium that is achieved between businesses and households necessarily has to be one where there is full employment of all resources available to the economy. It implies only that there will be an equilibrium between household earnings from the factor (labour) market and business earnings from the product (output) market, which can be attained at less than full employment.

In a complex economy, where many products are produced, a household need not purchase the products that it produces. In fact, it is almost certain that it will purchase other products out of the earnings it has received from producing one particular product. Taken across the whole economy, it would be remarkable that an exact match was achieved between the supply of products and demands for them.

Households change their tastes, leaving retailers with some products on their shelves, while for other products a queue might form. In a freely operating price system, excess supply in one product line would signal to the hirers of labour services, who manufacture that product, that they should hire less labour in the next production period; meanwhile, the hirers of labour services in the product lines in excess demand would receive signals from the existence of queues that they should expand production by hiring more labour.

These changes would not be instantaneous in the real world, and the time taken to allow the adjustments to work themselves through would cause a temporary disequilibrium between household incomes and business revenues (some households would find themselves holding cash balances in excess of their intentions, and some businesses would find themselves with unsold stocks of goods that they intended to sell).

This picture is all right for a simple two-sector circular flow economy, but what of the real world? Are there other factors that we should consider when trying to model what actually happens in real economies?

A French economist, who wrote at the turn of the nineteenth century, called Jean Baptiste Say, had the misfortune to fall out with the dictator Napoleon and have his books banned. He had the double misfortune to be credited with a crude version of a sound economic principle, namely, that 'supply creates its own demand'. What he in fact asserted was perfectly true: the sum of all demands in an economy is algebraically equal to the sum of all supplies.

If households earned income from selling labour services, they would try to spend those incomes on available supplies. If they could not buy what they had intended to buy, they would hold cash balances equal to their excess demands (i.e. the amount by which their demand exceeded supply) for those goods that they could not obtain, and suppliers would hold excess supplies (i.e. the amount by which their supply exceeded demand) of those goods that they could not sell. The algebraic sum of all the goods bought and sold plus the excess supplies of cash that households hold and the excess supplies that businesses cannot sell, will be zero. Prices must fall to clear the excess supplies of goods, thus mopping up the excess supplies of cash, and producers must re-adjust their outputs to produce what households want.

Say's principle does not imply that a given supply of something will create a demand for it, for that clearly would be a nonsense. Whether or not a demand is forthcoming for something will depend on the tastes of consumers and the price of the goods.

In the labour market itself, the mere fact of a supply of labour at current wage rates does not imply a demand for it by employers. If employers cannot envisage selling the output produced by the labour services of those seeking work, given the wages necessary to hire them, they will not hire their services. In case such actions by employers in refusing to hire unemployed workers is considered despicably anti-social, we must note that neither will consumers in households purchase goods merely because they are supplied.

Keynes latched on to the possibilities of disequilibrium between expenditures by households in product markets and their incomes from factor markets. He opened up the issue of a failure of household demand to match supply in the product markets. He dubbed the consequence of the behaviour of people failing to purchase current output of an economy a failure of *effective demand*. People were not spending enough on the goods and services that were produced to employ fully all those willing, and seeking, to work.

Employment is what economists call a *derived demand*. A business does not hire people for the sake of hiring them (though this may not apply to the practice of some government departments). They employ people because of the effective demand for the products that their labour services can produce.

For demand to be effective, rather than wishful or intentional, it must be backed by a *capability* to pay for the goods. The wishful demand for Rolls Royces greatly exceeds the effective demand for them.

If employers envisage an effective demand for their products that covers their costs, they will hire labour services to produce them. If effective demand falls, or does not materialise as planned, then employers will reduce their demand for labour services (i.e. sack employees); if effective demand is greater than anticipated or planned for, then employers will hire more labour services to produce more output.

What Keynes was interested in was not whether the economy would eventually adjust to reduce output where effective demand was lower than expected, or to increase output where effective demand was higher than expected, but whether there was a mechanism in an economy that would automatically ensure that effective demand would always be maintained close to the maximum output a given labour force and capital stock could produce.

In *The General Theory*, Keynes explained why he did not believe that such a mechanism existed in an economy left to itself. He went further; he asserted that in the circumstances of an economy left to its own devices, it is more likely that the economy will settle down at equilibrium states well short of full employment, and that there was no reason why it should (ever) settle at a full employment level in the absence of intervention to ensure that it did so. To see how he reasoned along these lines we shall have to look more closely at how he perceived that an economy, and its participants, households and businesses, actually operated.

Chapter 13

Consumption and saving

MOST PEOPLE MANAGE, without much effort, to spend their incomes, every last cent of them. The alternative of saving out of our incomes is not always the most common action for the majority of us. Yet save we do, as the national statistics show. People hold savings in bank deposit accounts, or have a specific amount deducted from each pay cheque for some purpose, often a pension fund, or they lend to a financial house of one kind or another (in Britain, a lot of people put their savings into building societies or into National, i.e. government, Savings Certificates). Some people draw the interest their savings earn as income to live on, others re-invest the interest in their savings to build up a 'nest egg' for 'a rainy day', or when they retire.

By the act of saving we are not consuming. We are *withdrawing* potential expenditure from the total stream of expenditures on household consumption goods and services. The proportion that households save collectively is of great importance to the functioning of the economic system.

If all income (Y) must either be consumed (C) or saved (S), we can write this statement in symbols as:

$$Y = C + S$$

In words this says: income is composed of consumption plus saving.

But if households save some of their incomes from selling labour services, how can businesses survive when they are not selling all their outputs of consumer goods and services? Moreover, if businesses cut their outputs, and therefore their demand for labour services, to match the reduced expenditure of those households that are saving part of their incomes, how can a household maintain its aggregate income if some of its members are being laid off by businesses?

Clearly, such a situation would be unstable if households continued to save out of their diminishing incomes, leading to a diminishing output from businesses, and consequently a diminishing demand for labour services, until there was no output at all and no employment.

Consumption by households is not, fortunately, the sole source of demand for the output of businesses. It has suited the exposition to this point not to emphasise the role of investment goods as a part of business ouput, but as we move deeper into economic analysis, and approach more realistic models of actual economies, we must introduce elements of the real world that complicate the simple picture so far presented here.

Investment goods are produced by businesses for other businesses. To invest in business activity requires a flow of financial services from households through financial intermediaries, such as banks. This flow of investment into the business sector is an *injection* into the system. This is illustrated in Fig. 6, as is the relationship between the savings from

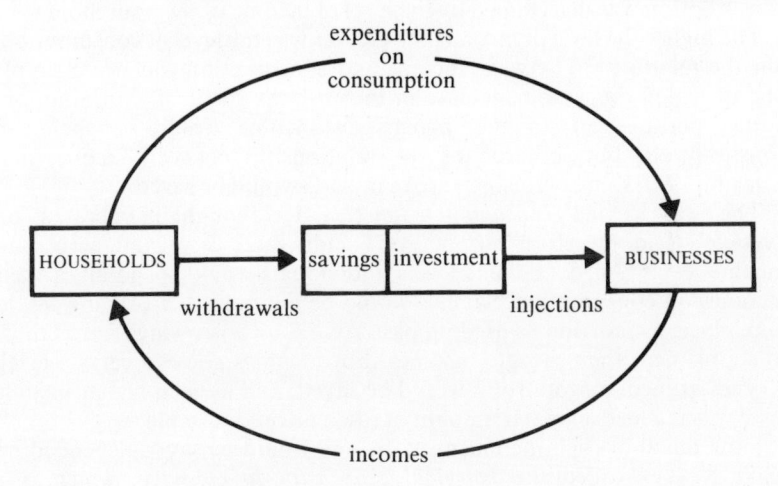

FIG. 6: Investment into the business sector

households (withdrawals from consumption expenditure) and investment into business (injections into the purchase of business output).

The flow of financial services into the business sector enables businesses to purchase business output for purposes of investment. The sum of purchases of output by households for consumption, and the purchases of output by businesses for purposes of investment, accounts for the total output of the business sector.

Business demand for investment goods can be added to the effective demand for consumption goods, reduced by household saving, to give total effective demand for business output.

The question that Keynes was interested in was whether the two sources of effective demand added together would necessarily be sufficient to ensure full employment output from business.

Clearly, it was possible for aggregate effective demand $(C + I)$ to equal total business output (i.e. $Y = C + I$). In other words, equilibrium income and output could be achieved, but whether this equilibrium was close to full employment output, or to some other lower level of output associated with high unemployment, was not obvious.

Additionally, questions as to what happened when disequilibrium existed – an imbalance between the withdrawal effect of savings and the injection effect of investment causing deficient effective demand below current output levels – and what caused this to happen, were also of great interest to economists investigating the phenomenon of prolonged unemployment experienced in the 1930s. It was in the answers to these questions that policy prescriptions for governments could be developed.

To tackle these questions, Keynes embarked on an investigation of the phenomenon of household consumption. He asserted that household consumption was determined by the level of income of the household.

The higher the level of income, the greater was the level of consumption, but the relationship between income and consumption was not a simple one in which every unit increase in income was spent on consumption. Some, perhaps all, of the increase in income would be spent on consumption, but, because of the relationship between income and consumption, some of the increase in income would be saved.

This was Keynes' *consumption function*. He thought it operated 'on average' (and therefore not in every individual case) and across all income levels. At low income levels, individuals would spend all of their incomes on consumption. Savings would be nil; indeed, *dis*-saving would take place, as individuals used up past savings or borrowings from others to supplement their meagre incomes. For incomes above a certain level, Keynes argued, a proportion would be saved, and as each higher income level was reached a greater amount of saving would take place.

How much of each increment in income would be saved depended on what Keynes called the *marginal propensity to consume*, which is a technical term for what is described more long-windedly in the previous paragraph!

If somebody's income went up $100, and he saved out of that amount $25, the marginal propensity to consume would be $75/100 = .75$ – three-quarters of each increment in income will be spent on consumption, and, by arithmetic, one-quarter of each increment in income will be saved. The proportion of each increment saved was called the *marginal propensity to save* (in this case 0.25).

So far, we have seen how income is spent either on consumption or on saving:

$$(Y = C + S)$$

The value of output is equal to the incomes paid out to produce it, and, therefore, output = income (in economics the symbol Y is used to represent *both* output and income).

Output is sold either for consumption or for investment:

$$(Y = C + I)$$

and by inspection of the two statements we can see that they have two terms in common (Y and C appear in both of them). It follows, on these arguments, that investment must equal saving ($I = S$) if the economic model is going to be in balance.

In addition, we have seen that Keynes believed that the proportion of shares of consumption and saving out of income was determined by what he called the consumption function. Keynes' consumption function is descriptive (i.e. it is what he believed happened in real world economies in the actions of millions of consumers) and not prescriptive (i.e. he was not recommending that it should happen).

Now, the question must be asked: what happens in the real world, and not just in our accounting arithmetic, when savings and investment are not equal to each other? And why on earth should they be equal?

The equality between saving and investment has to be brought about by the uncoordinated net result of the decisions, intentions and actions of many millions of individuals. It was asking for a high degree of coincidence for these actions to be so precisely balanced that the aggregate of savings by all households was exactly equal to the aggregate of investment by all businesses.

This coincidence was all the less likely, given that the people who did the saving out of their incomes were far more numerous than the people who made decisions about investment, there being far more consumers with incomes high enough to save than there are business entrepreneurs who make decisions as to whether and how much to invest.

Moreover, the decision to invest was not related, according to Keynes, to the level of income in the same way as the decision to save. Investment decisions are made by capitalist entrepreneurs and managers whose main concerns are with their expectations of making profits from their investments. What influences them and their expectations has more to do with their 'feelings' about the future, whether they are optimistic or pessimistic ('bullish' or 'bearish' as the slang of the money markets puts it), what they think will happen to interest rates and how these compare with their potential profit rates if they carried through the investment.

Casting your mind back to the concept of circulating capital and the item under this heading for 'finished products', you will recall that this referred to goods held in stock because they were not yet sold. Now consider the situation of the business manager, who has decided to purchase fixed capital assets, say, new machinery to expand output of a line of goods the company sells.

Typically, most investment programmes take time to come to fruition; it takes time to order the machinery, time to install it in a factory, time to get it into working order and time to produce output. In these (fairly typical and normal) conditions capital is being laid out by the business, and it could be years rather than months before the investment begins to earn a return. The delays between the decision to invest and the receipt of earnings from the investment will have been taken into account by the managers at the time they decide to make the investment (that, after all, is what they are paid for), but the fact that there is a delay indicates the precarious nature under which managers make these investment decisions – uncertainty about the future is an inhibiting influence on investment.

The decision to invest is taken on the best information available at the time the order is placed. By the time the machinery is operating, conditions for the product might have changed in the market place. As a consequence, the manager could find that the original investment decision was costing more than was *intended*, the extra cost being the result of having an increase in the stock of unsold finished products in the warehouse. These unsold stocks constitute *unintended* investment, and it is the sum of intended and unintended investment that makes up the amount actually invested at any one time.

If unintended investment appears, it indicates that consumers are saving more than was expected, for unintended investment, in the form of unsold stocks of goods, must perforce be matched by actual savings in the accounts of consumers. But the balance between saving and investment is not a balance between intended and unintended investment and saving. If it was, then we would be saying that businesses invest quite careless of whether they can sell their output or not, which we know not to be the case.

The balance between saving and investment is a balance between *intended* investment and saving, because businesses expect to sell the output arising from the investment at sufficient return to cover their costs and to make a profit.

Anything else would be suicidal for them, for it would mean making investments in projects that could not cover their costs because unintended unsold ouput has to be disposed of at a loss, or at prices that make it less than worthwhile going to the trouble, and risk, of undertaking an investment (they might as well keep their money in a bank and earn the current rate of interest).

This does not, however, resolve the problem of achieving a balance between the decisions of households to save out of their incomes, and the decisions of businesses to enter the financial services market in search of funds for intended investment.

The very actions of households deciding to save more out of incomes because they perceive a downturn in economic activity and they prudently wish to hold on to their funds for 'rainy days ahead', might provoke businesses into regretting earlier decisions to invest in new capacity, as their unsold output piles up in their warehouses, because households are buying less than businesses expected them to at some earlier date.

If businesses react to the recently-induced pessimism, they could retrench intended investment plans, reduce current capacity, and lay off employees. This reaction, while confirming the pessimism of those households that decided to increase their savings, will also have been caused by the appearance of that pessimism in the first place. It will also increase the atmosphere of pessimism in households and perhaps cause more caution in spending, which in turn will cause more pessimism among businesses and induce them to lay off yet more employees and curtail yet more investment plans. Before long, a full scale depression will be under way, induced in the first place by a mismatch between the actions of savers and the intentions of investors.

In reverse, perhaps in an outbreak of universal optimism as their warehouses run down their stocks and they think they can perceive a rush of consumers coming over the horizon with pockets and purses packed with cash, businesses could decide unilaterally as a group of decision makers to increase their intended investments. If they hire more employees from households, consumption spending will rise, confirming their optimism when this spending appears as effective demand in the shops. Saving will also be generated and this will match the intended investment of businesses. Falls in unintended investment (de-stocking of unsold goods) will induce more optimism and more planned investment, causing more employees to be taken on, with perhaps higher wages for those already working. The entire economy could move into, or towards, a boom.

We can see here a range of outcomes. Bust or boom at the extremes, balance in the middle, depending on whether actual savings are greater than, less than, or equal to, intended investment. That the economy can oscillate between the extremes, or more likely, oscillate about the middle, is at least a credible scenario. But absolutely nothing is present in the model we have described that suggests that equilibrium, even if obtained, would necessarily be an equilibrium close to full employment.

Having got his analysis into a working model, Keynes still faced the problem of that elusive goal of full employment output and income. To see how he tackled this problem, we need some more apparatus.

Chapter 14

The multiplier

THAT AN ECONOMY CAN BE IN EQUILIBRIUM but not at full employment is an important assumption of *The General Theory*. There is no 'law' of economics that causes the amount of output produced by an economy to be precisely the same as the amount of output that could be produced if everybody who wants to work is employed producing output.

Even if an economy was at full employment in March, it does not mean that it will be able to adjust its affairs such that it can be at full employment in June, if in the meantime the numbers looking for work have been substantially added to by the independent decisions of people joining or rejoining the working population (mothers deciding to rejoin the workforce as their children leave home, immigrants arriving at the frontier in search of refuge and work, previously sick people returning to work, and so on). But just because somebody, one morning, decides that he is going out in search of work instead of watching the grass grow, it does not follow that an employer has a vacancy for him that very same morning.

Clearly, all kinds of casual reasons can occur which cause individuals to decide that they want to join or remain in the workforce, and it would be an extremely refined economy that was able timeously to anticipate, with chilling precision, every whim, or necessity, of those who decide that they want to work at precisely the time that each makes his decision.

Full employment is one of many possible equilibriums for an economy, and, in many circumstances, it is not the most likely one to occur. When economic equilibrium occurs at substantially below the full employment output, it is a cause for political concern if this situation is prolonged, as the social tensions and stresses of large numbers of unemployed people threaten political stability.

Equilibrium occurs when what people desire to save out of their incomes is matched by what investors desire to invest in their businesses. If there is an imbalance between these two *desires*, savers and/or investors will be trying to conduct their affairs in a manner which will induce destabilisation of the existing equilibrium.

Far from collusion between savers and investors being a feature of equilibrium, it is the fact of the independence of their actions that produces equilibrium in the first place (we shall see how their actions are linked later), and out of this independence we get movements from one equilibrium position to another.

If savers desire to save more, or less, out of consumption this will set in motion economic forces that compel adjustments to be made in the production of national output until the amount that savers desire to save is brought back into balance with the amount that investors desire to invest. In this chapter we shall consider the processes by which these adjustments in national output are made.

Investment is the key variable that determines the amount of employment available for any level of national output. If national output varies, available employment will vary as well – the higher, of course, the amount of national output that is being produced the higher, other things being equal (i.e. in the short term with no changes in technology), the amount of employment that is available to households from businesses.

If employment is to increase, it is necessary for the amount of investment to increase above its current levels, and if this is to happen from a position of less than full employment equilibrium in the economy, it must mean that the amount of investment that businesses desire to undertake must exceed the amount that savers currently wish to save.

But, and this was an innovation in economic thinking when Keynes first included it in the *General Theory*, the amount by which investment increased to secure an increase in output was less than the amount by which output would increase as a result of that investment. In other words, for a given increase in investment there would be a greater increase in output, and thereby a greater increase in the derived demand for employment to produce the extra output.

When businesses decide to increase their investment in capital goods, they will perforce cause an increase in employment in the industries that produce those capital goods, for remember, employment is a derived demand and producers of capital goods, perceiving a rise in demand for their products, will hire more workers to produce those goods.

Keynes went beyond acknowledging an increase in demand for labour to produce extra investment goods. If the additional employment was confined to the response of manufacturers of investment goods there would be a one-for-one relationship between output and employment only. Employment, Keynes argued, would go up by much more than the initial (or, *primary*) injection of investment in acquiring capital goods, because the additional income earned by the newly hired employees in the investment goods industries would be spent on acquiring consumer goods for household purchases.

Hence, the effect of increasing investment by businesses was transformed by the consequential increase in consumption by households into an increase in demand for consumer goods and services, and this increase in demand would, in turn, increase employment in the consumer goods industries as employers responded to increased orders with an increase in their derived demand for labour services from households.

The cycle of increased derived demands for labour services would not cease at a 'single round', as the incomes of the newly hired workers added to household expenditures on business output; it would continue through several rounds until the initial injection of increased expenditures had worked itself through the system and brought about a new balance between saving and investment, albeit at a higher level of national output.

Keynes called this process the 'multiplier' and we can simultaneously illustrate it with a simple example and enhance our understanding of the meaning of equilibrium.

There are several elements of economic activity involved in the shift from one equilibrium to another. Investment is clearly one of them, so is consumption. The relationship between consumption and saving is crucial here, because it is out of the increased incomes of newly hired employees that consumption decisions are effected. How much of a household's income is spent and how much is saved will depend on the consumption function – the greater the proportion that is spent, the greater the amount of income this provides for those who sell goods and services to the household sector, and the greater the amount available in turn for these recipients to spend.

The marginal propensity to consume is the proportion of the amount of an increase in income that is spent. The proportion that is spent leaves a proportion that is saved, which is the marginal propensity to save. As there is no other way in which income can be disposed of besides that of consuming or saving, it follows that the marginal propensity to consume and the marginal propensity to save both sum to one.

If income (Y) is $100, and the household spends $80, then the marginal propensity to consume is $80/100 = 0.8$, or four-fifths. If $80 is spent it follows that $20 is saved, and thus the marginal propensity to save is $20/100 = 0.2$, or one-fifth. Out of every increase in income of $100, four-fifths will be spent and one-fifth will be saved. (Four-fifths plus one-fifth equals one.)

What happens when an economy experiences an increase in investment of $100? This becomes income to households who supply labour services (for simplicity we are ignoring complications about the division of the value added into wages and profits), and these households will spend $80 on consumption of goods and services. The businesses which supply the $80 of household consumption experience an increase in their incomes of $80. If, as we assume in our simple example, they will spend their additional incomes in the same proportions (80:20), they will spend four-fifths of the $80, which is $64, on consumption and save the rest ($16).

But the $64 that they spend is now income to those from whom they purchase their goods and services, and these people will also spend in the same ratio (80:20), providing incomes of $51.20 to the sellers of goods and services and adding $12.80 to savings. Each round of expenditure-income-expenditure shows a diminishing amount for expenditure and saving – by the third round the amount spent out of the original $100 investment injection has diminished from $80 to $51.20 – and this will gradually diminish towards zero. If, however, the amount spent in each round is added together you will find the series produces a total addition to consumption of around $400 and an addition to savings of $100, giving a total increase in national income of $500.

In Table 3 I show the rounds of multiplier in this example. There are two things to note about this series. Firstly, that the increase in national income is five times the original injection of $100 investment, and secondly, that five is the reciprocal of the marginal propensity to save of one-fifth. The arithmetic term, the *reciprocal*, is not an attempt on my part to impress you with mathematical symbolism; it is a shorthand way of indicating to you a significant economic relationship, namely, that the smaller the marginal propensity to save (i.e. the greater the marginal propensity to consume), the greater the multiplier effect of an initial injection of investment on national income.

TABLE 3: **Multiplier rounds for $100 injection**

Injection	*Consumption*	*Saving*
$100	$80	$20
80	64	16
64	51.2	12.8
51.2	41.0	10.2
41.0	32.8	8.2
32.8	26.0	6.8
26.0	20.8	5.2
...	...	...
...	...	...
500	400	100

For example, if the marginal propensity to save had been one half (0.5), giving a reciprocal of 2, the total effect on national income would have been to have increased it by twice the original injection of investment, i.e. $100 investment would have added $200 to national income. If, alternatively, the marginal propensity to save had been one tenth (i.e. nine tenths of each round of income was spent on consumption), the reciprocal would be 10, and national income would increase by ten times the original injection of $100, equals $1,000.

The amount by which the original injection increases national income is the Keynesian *multiplier*. The more people consume out of their incomes (the less they save) the more they add to effective demand, and the more, in consequence, they add to the derived demand for labour services or employment.

In a real world economy, the domestic multiplier effect of an investment injection will be countered by the existence of taxes on personal incomes (because these reduce the consumption effect of increased income), and by imports (because these add to consumption demand in foreign countries).

Note also, that in the multiplier rounds in our $100 example, the sum of the savings from each round was $100. Thus, the increase in investment, which we presumed was from an equilibrium position between saving and investment, has generated an increase in national income of $500 which, when the multiplier rounds are worked through, has produced an increase in desired savings of $100 to match the desired increase in investment of $100. Equilibrium has been established at a higher level of national income.

The connection between the increase in investment and the consequential increase in national output that generates both an increase in consumption (in our case of $400) and an increase in saving ($100) was of great significance to Keynes and his proposals to reduce unemployment in the midst of the 1930s depression.

If structural unemployment persists, it can be reduced towards the full employment level by injecting some amount of investment, calculated according to the country's actual multiplier.

In Britain's case, Keynes thought the multiplier was between 2 and 3 (because of heavy 'leakages' into taxation and imports), and on these grounds, if the gap between actual and full employment levels of national income was, say $2 billion, an injection of between $700 million and $1 billion would move the economy to full employment (because 3 times $700 million or 2 times $1 billion would close the gap of $2 billion).

The only agency that could contemplate investment injections on that kind of scale was, and remains, the government, and Keynesian economics has been associated with a major interventionary role of government ever since.

Chapter 15

Investment, interest and expectations

SO FAR, WE HAVE CONSIDERED THE ACT OF INVESTMENT without considering the factors that influence the amount that businesses desire to invest at any given moment. Investment is a normal activity in an economy and is undertaken by businesses according to their expectations about the future.

Investment is also a long-term activity. The rewards from an investment are not immediately achieved, and it takes time also to secure the return of the money originally invested.

Anything involving time involves risks; there are risks that the prospects for the investment do not materialise. If they do not, then the person who has made the outlay for the investment will suffer a loss; if they do materialise, then the person concerned will make a gain. It is the balance between the prospective gain and the risk of loss that tantalises the judgement of those who make decisions about business investment.

Households, to protect themselves from some risks of loss, will lend their savings at fixed (lower) rates of interest which are fairly certain to materialise, especially if loaned to a stable and reliable government, and forego the chance of a share in (larger) profits which are subject to greater degrees of risk.

Businesses are induced to allocate funds to the purchase of new productive capacity, by contrasting the prospective yield from investment and the cost of making the investment. This cost is the cost of borrowing the money to finance the investment, even if, as is the case sometimes, the actual money used for the investment comes from their own resources, such as past profits, and not from outside lenders such as banks.

The reason why the cost of borrowed money is used as the criterion of the cost of investment is simply that for a business, or indeed, a household, the alternative to the act of business investment in search of future profits is to lend the money to somebody else at an agreed rate of interest. If you can earn 10 per cent by placing your past profits with a bank, why should you undertake the much riskier, and perhaps more troublesome, activity of paying out your past profits to purchase a new factory that is likely, say, to return you only an 8 per cent rate of profit, even if everything went well and according to your plans?

Assuming that the bank is a soundly managed institution, and therefore less of a risk than a factory which has yet to be built and has yet to supply output that may or may not sell at a profit, you might just as well lend your money to the bank, earn at least the extra 2 per cent on your capital, and forego the hassle of setting up and managing a new factory.

If, alternatively, you expect a new factory to earn you profits in excess of 10 per cent, say, 20 or 30 per cent, you would be inclined to undertake the investment. In fact, in these circumstances, banks would also be looking for an opportunity to loan money, which they have borrowed at 10 per cent, to any well-managed business that wanted to borrow it for investment in this relatively profitable activity.

Overall, the level of investment in an economy will be influenced by the expectations of businesses regarding the prospective yields on new investments and the cost to businesses of borrowing money to finance the new investments.

Prospective yields, though often given a precise monetary value in a budget statement, remain subjective. The future is always uncertain, and Keynes in fact went to some considerable trouble to underline the nature of expectations about the future, especially regarding investment prospects.

Business entrepreneurs are compelled by uncertainty about the future to make a guess about what is likely to happen. If they get it right, and for bigger stakes, more often than they get it wrong, they will make bigger profits, or smaller losses, than those who perpetually guess wrong. Their incentive to get it right is the prospect of losing either their own money, or the ability to continue to use other people's money.

In this sense, they have a much greater personal stake in assessing the future yield on economic activity than, say, a salaried civil servant in a government Planning Ministry who invests taxpayers' money at little, or no, risk to himself. For this, and other reasons, individual risk taking in a capitalist economy is regarded as being more efficient than anonymous risk taking in a planned economy, and, on the evidence, capitalist-type economies are generally believed to show a higher and, therefore, more successful level of economic activity than socialist economies.

In modern economies, markets for investment funds exist, and consequential markets, such as stock exchanges, buy and sell the paper securities that represent invested funds. Moods of pessimism alternate, sometimes violently, with moods of optimism, and all kinds of subjective reactions to real events often push the prices of these equity securities in directions completely at variance with the actual prospective yields that influenced the original investors.

Keynes was more than a little critical of the gambling casino atmosphere of the stocks and shares market, but he understood thoroughly just how important were the 'animal spirits' of the business leader or entrepreneur. His 'recommendation' that the government take over long-term investment programmes, as well as engage in investment to raise economic activity to full employment levels, has sometimes coloured the reaction of non-socialist governments to his other prescriptions on the management of a modern economy.

If subjectivism rules in the case of prospective yields, what determines the cost of borrowing money? This boils down to discovering what determines the rate of interest. Rates of interest are quoted daily – sometimes, for some purposes, they are quoted every second or so – and are very real in this sense. Opinion as to what the rate of interest will be tomorrow, or next year, or throughout the lifetime of an investment project, are, of course, subjective and influenced by the same uncertainties as the yield on an investment.

The cost of the borrowed funds, however, is what they cost at the moment when they are borrowed. Hence, for our purposes we assume that the rate of interest will remain fixed for the borrower during the period of the loan, but you can readily imagine that the likelihood of fluctuating interest rates over the period of the loan adds a massive complication to any judgement about the prospective yield on an investment and the differential between a future uncertain yield and a future uncertain rate of interest. This would take us, however, into the fascinating subject of financial economics and away from our immediate concerns.

The rate of interest is simply the price of borrowing money, and for different borrowing purposes there are different rates of interest. In macroeconomics we speak of *the* rate of interest but this should not cause any untoward confusion as long as we remember that the purpose of our economic models is to represent the real world and not reproduce it.

Money is one way in which an individual can hold his or her wealth. Money represents a claim on economic goods and services, and each individual is under no obligation to present immediately his or her claims on available goods and services at the precise moment that he or she acquires his or her money. They can choose to keep some proportion of their wealth in the form of money, and some other proportion in the form of real goods.

People are influenced by various motivations for holding money: the need to carry cash to make purchases; the need to hold cash just in case something unforeseen happens to them; and the need to have money available in case they see an opportunity for making a profit. Keynes called these, respectively, the *transactions*, the *precautionary* and the *speculative*, motives.

The actual amount of money (defined as cash and current bank accounts which do not yield interest) a person has to hand at any one moment will depend upon his or her income (mainly) and the rate of interest. The richer I am the greater my daily expenditures and the more cash I need to meet them. The transactions and precautionary motives for holding money are more sensitive to my income level than they are to the interest rate.

The speculative motive for holding money is more likely to fluctuate according to the opportunities for making a profit, which adds to future income, than it is to the level of current income. The rate of interest has a large influence on the amount of cash held for this purpose.

If interest rates are relatively high, they are likely to encourage individuals to place their spare (speculative) cash balances with borrowers; if they are relatively low, the reverse is likely to happen and individuals are likely to increase their holdings of cash instead.

The tendency to hold wealth in the form of money Keynes called *liquidity preference*, for cash is the most liquid of all assets. By liquid, we mean the ability to transform our money wealth into any economic goods we can afford in the shortest possible time.

Consider a less liquid form of holding our wealth. If we have purchased a building, in order to keep our wealth in the form of bricks and mortar, rather than for purposes of using the building to live or work in, and if, for any reason, we need or want to acquire cash, we can decide to sell the building for cash. To do this we have to notify potential buyers, negotiate a price if we find a buyer, and then exchange the building for the buyer's cash.

This takes time, and the longer it takes – suppose we cannot immediately find a buyer because everybody with cash wants to keep his wealth in the form of cash – the less liquid is our asset. With cash, we can immediately make any transaction we can afford, and if we prefer to increase our cash holdings for any reason we are said to have a high liquidity preference.

The price of borrowed money, like the price of any other economic good, is determined by the demand and the supply of money. People demand to hold money, for reasons stated above, according to their desire for liquidity. But what of the supply of money? Who or what determines this?

In a modern economy, the government determines the supply of money, and we shall examine this in much greater detail later. For the moment, we can assume that governments, through the central or main bank, determine the amount of money in the economy (after all, governments print the banknotes and stamp the coins with a likeness of its leader, or with some other symbol of nationhood).

If, for the present, we take the amount of money in the economy as fixed by the government, we can see that the variable factor is the liquidity preference of the community. At high interest rates the community prefers to hold interest-earning assets rather than non-interest earning cash, and, therefore, less money will be demanded than at low interest rates when the penalty for holding money rather than cash is less onerous. Where the demand for money, given by liquidity preference, is equal to the supply of money, given by government policy, a rate of interest will be established.

Now, since the rate of interest influences the decision of business investors to undertake investment in new capital goods, and since the undertaking of investment, through the multiplier, determines the level of national income, it can be seen that the ruling rate of interest influences the level of economic activity.

If the level of economic activity is in equilibrium at less than full employment, and the government wants to raise activity towards full employment, it can do so, according to Keynesian economics, by reducing the rate of interest. This will encourage business investors to undertake investment projects they are presently dissuaded from undertaking because of the prospective yield from new investments compared with the ruling rate of interest.

Unfortunately, the situation is not always so clear-cut. While, in general, it is true that reductions in the rate of interest would encourage businesses to undertake new investment projects, there are situations, especially in prolonged depressions, where a policy of reducing the rate of interest is likely to be frustrated by the fact that interest rates are already regarded as being relatively low. To see this, remember that at low interest rates people prefer to keep their wealth in the form of cash, and at very low interest rates some people will not be induced to part with their cash, and thereby become less liquid, in favour of investment projects that may take some years to come to fruition.

Keynes called this possibility the *liquidity trap*, and when such a trap existed, something more than a reduction in interest rates was needed to get the economy growing again. He suggested that the government would have to step in and undertake major investment projects, or *public works*, in the absence of businesses who, because of their pessimistic expectations of the future, were not responding to lower interest rates in pursuit of profitable investment opportunities. If they feared to invest, because of the threat of losses, and individuals preferred to hold cash rather than real goods, it was not possible for the depression to be ended and the economy moved towards full employment equilibrium in the absence of direct government intervention.

Keynes was scathing in his condemnation of those economists who persisted with awaiting for 'natural' economic forces to work their way through and pull the economy out of a depression. He did not believe that individual businesses, especially in a deep and prolonged depression, where expectations were severely dampened down by prospective losses rather than yields, had sufficient foresight, or reserves, to spend their way back towards full employment. He thought it would require monumental courage on the part of individual businesses, with their relatively short time horizons, to generate enough new investment to move towards lower unemployment levels through the multiplier.

Governments, on the other hand, had longer time horizons, and much greater economic endurance. Their only problem, as he saw it, was an addiction to incorrect economic theories. He went much further, and waxed lyrical (as was, apparently, his personal style!) on the absurdities that nonsensical economic theories imposed on those who accepted them.

He argued that it did not really matter what public works were funded, or what principles of enterprise were involved in carrying them out. Naturally, in his view, common sense suggested that useful public works were better than useless ones, but if what was useful was not possible for reasons of political prejudice (perhaps, for example, an aversion to publicly-provided housing) then he advocated that politically neutral, though useless, projects be undertaken instead.

For instance, Keynes suggested, not too seriously, in the *General Theory* that the government could bury at the bottom of disused coal mines, using town refuse, old bottles filled with banknotes, and then employ private businesses to dig them up again! The economic effects of the expenditures involved, through the multiplier, would be the same as a really worthwhile public programme (he suggested housebuilding).

As a result of this government funded investment programme, employment would rise, national output and incomes would rise, the expectations of businesses would be revised optimistically and from this a self-sustaining level of economic activity would be enjoyed.

With such obvious benefits available, it might be wondered why it took so long for Keynesian policies to be tried, and, given that they were associated with the long boom years 1945–73, why they are not being applied today with unemployment in the industrialised economies once again approaching 1930s levels. We shall pursue these questions in the following chapters.

Chapter 16

Fiscal policies

IF ECONOMIC MANAGEMENT was as straightforward as a sympathetic reading of *The General Theory* of 1936 suggests, the question might well be put: why hasn't it happened?

Surely, if effective demand is not high enough to ensure full employment output, a government has the economic power to intervene by increasing its own expenditures, or, what amounts to a similar thing, reducing its taxes on households and businesses so that they can increase their expenditures? Conversely, if effective demand is too high to ensure stable prices, why can't governments either reduce their own expenditures or, what amounts to a similar thing, increase taxes on households and businesses so that they are compelled to reduce their expenditures?

The actions suggested above – altering government expenditures and taxes – amount to *fiscal* policy to regulate aggregate demand. If government expenditure (G) is increased, this adds to private business investment (I); if government taxes (T) are reduced, this adds to private consumption (C), and both add to aggregate demand:

$$(Y - T = C + I + G).$$

In the face of unemployment, a government following Keynesian fiscal policies would increase its expenditures from G to G^1, and the addition to aggregate demand ($G^1 - G$) would stimulate the economy through the multiplier in exactly the same way as an increase in investment from I to I^1.

With a low marginal propensity to save, the economy might approach full employment with a relatively small increment in government expenditure. This increment in government expenditure would be funded by the government going into deficit, i.e. its expenditures (G) would exceed taxation (T).

Alternatively, or in some combination with an increase in G, the government could increase private consumption (C) by tax cuts. This would increase the amount of disposable income (Y) available for consumption. The higher the marginal propensity to consume, the more immediate the economic effect of a tax cut. Net-of-tax income would go up, and households could be expected to spend some (high) proportion of the increase in disposable income on current goods and services, stimulating the household consumer goods industries to raise output and, through this, to raise employment.

Which combination of fiscal policies a government would choose to manage aggregate demand would depend on various factors. This was demonstrated, though not with Keynesian intentions, at the outbreak of the Second World War of 1939–45. Governments dramatically increased their expenditures to produce war materials (an increase in $G^1 - G$ on an unprecedented scale!) and, in conjunction with mass mobilisation into the armed services of millions of male soldiers, the high levels of 1930s structural unemployment very rapidly diminished towards frictional levels. Indeed, so dramatic was the turn round, that the main concern of economists, with Keynes to the fore in 1939, soon switched from worries about deficient demand and unemployment to worries about excessive demand and inflation!

The switch from policies to counter unemployment to policies to counter inflation was containable within *The General Theory* (it would hardly have been describable as a *general* theory if it could not cope with the phenomenon of inflation). Keynes cautioned against attempting to increase investment 'still further' when full employment is reached, because to do so 'will set up a tendency for money-prices to rise without limit'.

Inflation, in this Keynesian model, is caused by an excess of effective demand over full employment output. Households, businesses or the government, or perhaps all three sectors together, are trying to consume more than is available from full employment output. There is, what Keynes called, an *inflationary gap*, as opposed to a *deflationary gap* when structural unemployment exists. The excess demand for goods and services will not cause an increase in output – for no increase is possible at full employment with existing labour services and capital stock – but will manifest itself in rising prices. Increased prices will both deter some would-be consumers from purchasing goods, and reduce the income available for the purchase of other goods among those who pay the higher prices for existing output.

In his classic essay *How to Pay for the War* (first published as articles in *The Times*), Keynes advocated an ingenious system of deferred taxation on wartime personal earnings, which would reduce high and potentially inflationary wartime aggregate demand to full employment output. It would achieve this by temporarily reducing household consumption through deliberately raising taxes, and then, after the war, some of these taxes would be repaid as tax credits and spent by households. In this way aggregate demand would be maintained at the full employment output after the war as government military purchases were reduced to peacetime levels.

As it happened, post-war aggregate demand remained sufficient to sustain full employment, and a Keynesian-type tax credit system was not necessary (in contrast with the experiences of the immediate post-war years after the 1914–18 war, when severe economic depression afflicted the former war-combatants when peace returned to Europe).

Keynesian demand management in conditions of near full employment required what politicians like to call 'fine tuning', which gives, perhaps, an altogether far too precise impression of the actual possibilities open to governments who seek to influence aggregate demand in a modern industrialised economy.

This problem is compounded when the full impact of government spending is appreciated. Take, for instance, the case where a government is strictly balancing its books, that is, it is spending only what it takes from households in the form of taxation ($G = T$), and it is neither borrowing nor engaging in deficit financing of its own expenditures. Government expenditure in these circumstances is not *neutral*, for a balanced budget can be expansionary.

The money taken from households in taxation is spent by the government, maintaining, in effect, the level of household consumption (if you like, taxation shifts income from one group of consumers to another group of newly employed consumers who are now working on government contracts). But government expenditures add to aggregate demand and the GNP is increased accordingly at a new higher equilibrium level. National output will expand until the amount injected as government expenditure is 'paid for' by the increased amount taken in taxation from the newly employed households, in much the same way as private investment generates the savings to pay for it out of an increased national income.

This leads to a problem for an economy operating a Keynesian type demand management fiscal policy. If, close to full employment, even a balanced budget tends to expand national output, inflationary pressures must be induced by a government merely balancing its budget. While these inflationary pressures are less than they would be if the government attempted to continue a fiscal policy of deficit financing, they are nevertheless real enough to promote some fears that inflationary pressure may be generated by any government intervening in an economy close to full employment that is not at the same time running a surplus, i.e. a situation where taxes are greater than government expenditure.

The countervailing pressure to the control of inflation in a democracy (or in a dictatorship that is 'running scared') is the pressure from households for continually rising living standards, either as wages for labour services (so-called 'cost push') or as increased benefits from government expenditure in the form of the social wage ('free' public goods – health, education, subsidised foods, etc.).

The western democracies in the post-1945 period have certainly experienced constant pressure from trade unions and official incomes commissions of one kind or another for annually rising money wages, and they have also experienced rising real expenditures by governments on 'merit' goods, such as are provided by a welfare state.

To be fair, governments of all political colours have tended to respond to these pressures with election promises and commitments that preclude, effectively, a reduction in government spending below the amount taken in taxation. This has meant that many governments have actually run spending deficits, even at activity levels close to full employment.

In combination, it may be that the pressures to maintain government budgets at deficit spending levels, for wholly laudable reasons, may have contributed considerably to long-running western inflation levels, and to public expectations regarding the levels of public expenditure, which in sober calculation might be considered beyond the current economic means of the countries concerned.

This has made it nigh impossible to do more than cut the rate of increase in public expenditure in most western economies, let alone reduce the absolute total of public expenditure. Countries, such as France, Britain and the United States, have had governments which have pursued, or rather attempted to pursue, without success so far, policies of absolute reductions in public expenditure in, sometimes near desperate, efforts to reduce government spending to at least the balanced budget position.

If determined discretionary action has been unable so far to reduce government spending to eliminate deficits, there seems to be little hope of inflation being curbed beyond current levels by these means, and this might account for higher than normal levels of unemployment being experienced in many industrialised countries. Unable to effect a reduction in inflation by eliminating government deficits, the government may be forced into trying to curb household incomes by high levels of unemployment. The issues, and the debate, remain contentious, and we shall return to them in later chapters.

One of the advantages claimed for a well-organised fiscal system is that a 'built-in' regulator can be applied to the economy that does not require the conscious intervention of a government department, but which can act as a 'self correcting' mechanism for an economy experiencing cyclical movements in its level of activity.

A built-in stabiliser works automatically, and a taxation system designed to do so contributes, it is argued, to economic stability. In the upswing of the business cycle, as businesses experience boom conditions and can sell all they can produce, a progressive taxation system (one that takes a larger slice of income in taxation at each pre-determined level of income) acts to dampen down tendencies to move from manageable boom to outright inflation.

The higher the incomes that are earned in these conditions, the greater the levels of household taxation, and these reduce disposable incomes below what they would be if taxes were merely in the same proportion for all levels of income. At very high levels of income, taxation would rise faster and slice off successively higher levels of income before the household could attempt to spend all that it earned. This restrains household incomes close to the full employment output and reduces inflationary pressures.

In contrast, as a boom gives way to depression, smaller proportions of taxation are taken from disposable incomes, until, at some pre-determined level, no income tax is payable at all. This creates a floor through which the economy is prevented from falling at lower levels of national income.

Any additional allowances or social security payments that are made to the unemployed also strengthen the anti-recessionary floor. Where these are paid by statute – entitlement is determined by status only – they shore up the slowdown in economic activity above the level to which it might fall in their absence.

Contrawise, as unemployed households get back to work in the upswing of the boom, their statutory social security payments cease to apply and this dampens the inflationary effects of their moving on to higher income levels.

It was argued for a long time, by critics of Keynesian fiscal policy, that too much discretion was left to governments, who not only were unreliable – because they gave in to special interests rather than resist them in the quite understandable desire to remain in office – but also they were not all that good at demand management even if it was needed.

By the time the government noticed and agreed that some fiscal adjustment was needed ('a touch on the tiller' was how one British Prime Minister described what his fiscal policy was intended to do), and by the time they were able to make the adjustment, the policy came into effect too late to handle the originally perceived problem, and often, perversely, began to have an influence of a countervailing nature.

By then the government might decide that something else needed to be done and was already planning to intervene in another direction. This led the critics to suggest that so-called government-managed 'fine tuning' was actually a brutally blunt instrument. Discretionary interventions were applied too late and with too much impact, and they actually destabilised more than they stabilised. In sum, Keynesian interventions made things worse.

The critics (some of whom we shall meet in later chapters on monetarism) supported non-discretionary built-in stabilisers that worked automatically and without the decision lags of the kind experienced by discretionary interventions. With the latter, even if a decision could be made quickly as to what to do, it was more than likely to be too heavy or too light-handed to be much good.

With a built-in stabiliser, this was avoided. It began to operate timeously, because those who required, or ceased to require, an automatic right to assistance received or lost it automatically without bureaucratic delays, and with just the right amount of economic impact, because entitlements were decided beforehand and were based on the best assessments of what was needed in whatever economic circumstances the individuals concerned found themselves.

It must be said, however, that so-called Keynesian demand management policies (discretionary and non-discretionary), which were supposedly in operation throughout the boom years of 1945–73, were not conspicuously successful instruments for managing industrialised economies. Various policies of demand management were pursued, for instance in the United Kingdom, involving either fiscal policies that adjusted the taxation levels to 'squeeze out' inflationary tendencies, or various kinds of 'incomes and prices' policies aimed at restraining upward-only wage and price changes.

The continuing growth in government expenditures throughout these years, almost irrespective of the actual level of aggregate demand present in the economy, and often complicated by problems with the balance of payments, maintained high levels of aggregate demand, and therefore of incomes, which brought with them inflationary pressures that grew in scope until they became the dominant economic problem of the last twenty years.

The current situation of high levels of unemployment *and* inflationary pressures have, in effect, paralysed, where they have not discredited, the Keynesian remedies of aggregate demand management.

Alternative policies with wider appeal to governments concentrated on inflation rather than unemployment as the key economic problem. These policies, known generically as *monetarism*, became the predominant policy instrument in the industrialised countries of Europe and North America, and replaced, to a greater or lesser extent, Keynesian fiscal policies for demand management. That they have not (yet) produced the economic results promised by their advocates has added to the controversies surrounding their adoption by elected governments in the 1980s.

PART III Chapter 17

The non-monetary economy

SO FAR WE HAVE TALKED ABOUT MONEY as if there were total agreement on what it was and why it exists. Using the term 'money', in our context, is not too great a burden on your understanding because readers of this book will have handled money at some time or other and will have, therefore, an intuitive understanding of what it does, or is meant to do, and what it means to be without it, or to have less of it than you need for a particular purchase.

One of the problems with some attempts to develop a theory of money is the tendency for their authors to forget the simple, common-sense, notion of the role of money, and to develop instead some highly abstract (and often totally unrealistic) complications. We shall try to avoid abstract theorising and will stick to a simplified exposition of the role of money in an economy. This will not save you from the controversies about money in economics, but will prepare you better for coping with them in later chapters.

Let us suppose we lived in a fairly complex economy that did not have money, but instead arranged for all transactions between people to be based on the principles of direct *barter* (the exchange of one good for another in a single transaction). What would such an economy look like?

As we humans have progressed from the simple hunter-gatherer society, to become shepherds and farmers, and, as our needs and life-styles have become more complex, from small village life to large towns and eventual urban industrialisation, we have raised our living standards, and reduced our self-sufficiency. The *loss* of self-sufficiency from producing for ourselves almost everything that we needed, to requiring that almost everything be got for ourselves in exchange, has been matched by the *gain* in our living standards.

We have become more dependent upon each other to produce the ever widening range of goods and services that constitute our living standards, and, by becoming more interdependent, we require, in consequence, to develop systems of exchange.

An economy is complex if the participants are a long way from being self-sufficient and have to trade with others to acquire goods that they do not (cannot) produce for themselves. Each participant produces something that can be traded for the things that he wants, assuming that each can find somebody else willing to barter for what each produces.

This presents the first problem of a barter economy: matching people with goods to trade. If you produce, say, water from a well on your land, and require everything else that you consume from others, you will offer your water in exchange to those who want your water and are willing to trade for it for the goods that you want.

Either they must come to you beside your well in search of a trade for water, or you must take your water to them. You might have to place it in containers and hawk it around the neighbourhood while looking for those willing to trade their spare food, clothing, household goods, replacement containers, if yours are wearing out, and perhaps carts and camels to pull them or imported engines to drive them, and all the other things that you might wish to consume, assuming, of course, that there is a large enough market for your water to enable you to aspire to such living standards.

I have chosen the example of water as the product of your labour efforts, but it could just as easily be anything else, and, in a developed economy it might be of such a highly specialised nature that you will be involved in a relatively long, and no doubt weary, search for somebody looking to trade his food, say, for your steel metric sized spanners (too bad if you find only customers for USA sized spanners).

Whatever the degree of complexity of your product, your trading activities (the search for potential trading partners, and then haggling with them over the rate of exchange) will cost you time and effort to complete. If you have to do this every day, your searches and bargaining activities (known as *transaction costs*) will take up varying amounts of time and effort, which will reduce the time available for producing the items that you have for trade. This will be particularly so if the persons who might want to trade with you change every day and your search for them suffers from inefficiencies, such as if, when you are in their part of town looking for them, they happen to be searching for a trading partner in your part of town. It would be just as bad if each of you waited in your own part of town for the other to come looking for a deal!

In the barter economy as a whole, the transaction costs of search and haggle could be substantial, with hours, even days, taken up in fruitless searches for trading partners who just happen to want what you are offering and in the quantities that you have available at the time that you contact them. Moreover, the problem is doubly compounded by the necessity that *both* of you simultaneously want exactly what each has to offer, and that you both want it in exactly the same trading proportions that each of you considers a fair 'price' for your products.

If you want to trade fifty litres of water in a container for a horse, and he wants only twenty litres of water, and anyway would not trade a horse for so little, how do you complete the transaction? You could haggle all day and still not get a deal, even though the scope for a deal is extensive (how about twenty litres of water now, followed by another thirty litres next week?).

The problems of divisibility of each other's products and of finding people with matching desires, make bartering an inefficient system of trading. It might be possible to reduce some costs by arranging for everybody with something to trade to meet in a selected place on a specific day – the original 'marketplace' – and thus concentrate all the searches in one place. This simplifies the problem of searching but does not necessarily reduce the haggling between potential trading partners.

To complete some transactions will still require that partners find exactly the right combination and sequence of transactions that lead them from one transaction to another, with exactly the matching combinations of what they have to sell for what they want to buy.

Inevitably, in such a market, and in a bid to reduce the divisibilities problem, traders will tend to sell their produce in trade for other tradable goods, such that they trade large quantities of their own goods for quantities of other goods in excess of their immediate needs, and having secured the quantities of the other goods that they need, will add the surpluses of those goods to their own tradable good.

If you can trade four of your five containers of water for a horse, ten bags of flour, a set of ten chairs and ten copies of 'The Barterer's Yearbook', you can reserve the horse, five bags of flour, four chairs and a copy of the yearbook, and stay in the market place looking for traders who want any of your available water, and from one to six chairs, one to five bags of flour, and one to nine copies of the yearbook.

In other words, you have extended your potential opportunities of trading in the market, from people who want only water, to customers who might want water with combinations of other things. By having more potential traders with whom you can do deals, you might increase the opportunities for getting the remaining items that you require, in exchange for your original offering of five containers of water, a lot more quickly than trying to line up a specific sequence of deals that might, or might not, achieve the same object.

In fact, by building up stocks of goods from other producers, and having them available for instant inspection and trade, you could gradually get out of the water business and specialise as a general trader in the country's market place, willing to trade anything for anything.

Your customers would not have to search as diligently to find an exact matching trade for their goods. They could call on you first and see what deals you were offering, perhaps for all of their produce in one large deal that enabled them to take in exchange from you various amounts of different goods that you have traded from other people.

The presence of general traders in a barter market would be another step towards reducing the transaction costs of trading. The market could, in effect, change from a sequence of individually arrived-at bilateral barter deals into a general barter market. General traders would act as middle-men between the bulk sellers of specific produce and the individual purchasers of smaller quantities of numerous products.

The frequency with which individual purchasers offered to exchange their produce for varying combinations of the goods available in the general store, would lead to more or less obvious and semi-permanent 'price' lists – ten litres of water, say, will 'buy' you any one of the following items: a coat, a bag of rice, two sets of knives and forks, four water bottles, half a dozen kilos of dates, an annual subscription to the national newspaper, a ten course meal, a servant's services for a month, a tyre for your truck, etc.

The innovation of a barterer's price list would itself be very cumbersome, for what it 'saves' in the time taken to haggle it might lose in time taken to scrutinise the immense detail it would require. Every single item that was likely to be traded would have to have its rate of exchange, or price, listed against every other single item. If there were only 100 items available for trade there would still be 4,950 individual 'prices' of each item for every other one. The trader's walls would be covered with 'price' lists, and any changes in prices due to changes in taste, supply, demand, quality, the season, and any other influence, including those of a totally arbitrary nature, would require to be posted as amendments that were consistent right across the 100 items.

If a price difference between coffee and dates appeared that was not reflected in the price of coffee in terms of handbags and handbags in terms of dates, it would soon provoke *arbitrage* by a sharp-eyed trader. Such a trader is to be found in all markets and that is why some traders soon become richer than others, and he would sell dates for handbags and buy coffee with the handbags; he would then sell the coffee for dates at an extra profit, until, that is, the original, but not too wide awake, general trader spotted what was going on and amended his price list to show consistent prices between coffee, dates and handbags.

Could trading be improved in efficiency even further? Yes. By the innovation of *money*.

If the traders could agree on using one good that will be exchanged for all and any good, they can reduce the costs of search and haggling to a minimum, and it does *not* matter, for the monetary function of the good, which good they choose, providing they all agree explicitly, and by their behaviour, to which good to give the role of money, though some goods have better characteristics than others in the role of money.

By adopting a good as money, they reduce the pricing problem to one of fixing each good in terms of the *money* good, and by allowing people to sell their produce for the money good only, and leaving it to them to purchase what they want with divisible amounts of the money good for any and all of the products in the market, they simplify trading transactions immeasurably.

Instead of a price list of every product in terms of every other product, they simply price each good in term of the money good (reducing the price list from 4,950 prices for 100 items to 100 prices only).

When you take your five containers of water to market, you know that you will get money for the water, and you know also that the money will buy for you the other goods that you require. Instead of an extensive search for a trading partner, you can sell your water for the money good, still haggling if you wish on its price in money, and then work your way through a shopping list for the other goods that you want, using your money to purchase them.

When Captain Cook visited Tahiti in the eighteenth century, he traded iron nails for water, food and artifacts belonging to the Tahitians. The local inhabitants had never seen metals before and very quickly learned how to batter iron into more lethal spearheads and knives than the wooden ones they had used up to then.

So successful was trading in iron nails between the Tahitians and European visitors, that one captain had to take stern measures to stop the trade because his seamen were stealing the nails out of the ship's planking and his ship was in danger of capsizing! But, by instituting a trading post (literally by a designated tree close to the shore) that priced all the local goods in nails, Captain Cook, and others who followed him, simplified the task of acquiring local produce on a voluntary traded basis, which also had the side-effect of ensuring peace and harmony between the local inhabitants and the uninvited visitors.

Another important feature of using money as a trading good, that has immense implications for economic activity, is the fact that you can choose to take back home with you the money you have received from selling your water and wait for a more propitious time to spend it on goods that you need. The money good is not just a means of making *transactions*, it is also a *store* of purchasing power, enabling you to separate your sales activities from your purchasing activities, if inclination and circumstance suggest that this is in your interests.

The use of money is not a totally cost-free activity. There are, sometimes substantial, costs in using just any good as money. For example, if the chosen money good is relatively bulky or difficult to handle (such as the large round stones used by some Pacific islanders), the tendency would be to spend it there and then to avoid having to transport it home and look after it when you got it there. If it requires a lot of attention (feeding, if the money good is camels or horses, or, as has been the case in history, slaves), you would have to consider this as an expense against the potential purchasing power of your stored money. The longer you keep money goods that are perishable, unless fed or maintained in some way, the more your original unspent purchasing power will diminish through time.

Much better if the good chosen as money is *portable*, does not require expenditure on your part to maintain it (except, inevitably, the costs of safeguarding it from thieves), and is acceptable for purchases irrespective of how long you wihhold it from the market.

The history of money has been a long progression of money goods becoming more portable, easily divisible, and extensively acceptable to all citizens in the economy. To guarantee general and universal acceptability of the chosen money good or standard, it has been the practice for governments to take over the entire production of the money good and to enforce its acceptance by law.

The positive advantages of government-backed money are numerous, and we shall examine them next, alongside the disadvantages that include interventionary activities in money markets for political rather than for economic objectives.

Chapter 18

The monetary economy

NUMEROUS GOODS HAVE FUNCTIONED AS MONEY since it was first discovered (and independently re-discovered through many civilisations and societies) over the centuries. In a pastoral society, the obvious money good was sheep, or horses, or cattle or camels. In some places, coral shells have acted as money, so have salt, heavy stones, beads, nails, cigarettes, rum and paper.

In the nineteenth century, a French opera singer gave a concert on one of the Pacific islands and received in payment a third share of the takings, which turned out to be: three pigs, twenty-three turkeys, forty-four chickens, five thousand coconuts, and numerous bananas, lemons and oranges. It is not reported what she did with this unusual (to her, not to the islanders) mode of payment, but she did calculate that her fee was worth in Paris about 4,000 francs.

When the British established their penal colony in Australia in 1788, they sent out several hundred convicted 'criminals', accompanied by soldiers to guard them. Everything was included in the fleet sent out to establish the prison colony, *except money*! The omission made some sense because it was intended that the prisoners would work to produce their own food, clothing and shelter, and to provide the same for their guards. There was no need, in the official, and in the event, very naive, view, for money in a prison colony. The soldiers would be paid in cash when they returned from their tour, as Britain was the only place where they could actually spend their wages, and as most of the prisoners would be most unlikely ever to return to the UK they would not need money at all.

Prisons, today, are run in such a way that officially they do not require an *internal* monetary system for the bulk of their activities. The prison authorities decide who shall work and what rations are to be made available. Purely nominal wages can be earned for certain types of work, and the loss of even this nominal income, and the much larger non-monetary privileges, including normal quantities of food, etc., act to deter misbehaviour. There is an unofficial, and illegal, system run by the 'tobacco barons' who gain informal privileges and money debts (redeemed outside the prison by associates) from other prisoners who want to smoke.

For some years, in the absence of a political administration, the officers of the British regiment sent to guard the Australian colony in

Sydney set up a trading monopoly with the outside world, using their own pay credits which were cumulating in London as a means of paying visiting ships, whose owners had a use for money only in Britain (there was nothing for them to buy in the penal colony). The captains of the ships on their return to London took the officers' 'notes of payment' to the Army pay offices and cashed them for British money.

The officers, meanwhile, re-sold the imported cargoes at large profits to their soldiers (against their undrawn pay waiting in London), to members of the government administration of the colony, and to the few independent settlers.

The colonial government, on the other hand, bought locally produced corn from the independent settlers to feed the prisoners and the soldiers. Prices were fixed in bushels of locally produced corn, and settlers issued debtors' notes denominated in bushels of corn. The price of corn was related to prevailing values in British currency, and the basis for a monetary system was established, even though no actual money was available in the colony.

Corn was produced locally, but the army officers did not control the corn, which was grown by the independent settlers and sold directly to the government. All visiting ships had to report to the military before landing any cargoes and the military forced each ship to sell all its cargo, including casks of rum, under threat of refusing to let it land anything at all. Thus, their monopoly of trade enabled the army officers to establish imported rum, which they did control, as a rival form of money, instead of corn which they did not.

The rum trade was also very profitable. What cost a few shillings for the officers to buy from passing ships, they re-sold for up to 30 shillings a pint on shore. Those who consumed the rum, to relieve, perhaps, their treatment or their despair at never returning to their native land, ensured it remained in scarce supply.

Eventually, almost everything was priced unofficially in pints of rum, and the officers grew very rich as a result of managing both the imports of goods that people were desperate to consume, and the supply of the only 'money' available for purchasing those goods for the majority of people in the colony.

They paid their own men, in the form of pints of rum (at a small discount against their army pay held in London) which the soldiers could either consume or sell at a profit to prisoners. As some prisoners were anxious to acquire rum, perhaps for re-sale to fellow prisoners, or to purchase extra goods from the official stores at high prices, they offered to work extra days for local settlers or the army. This made it essential for settlers to acquire rum to pay for the extra work they needed.

Rum, as money, existed alongside corn during the early years of the colony, until, eventually, by their abuse of economic power, the entire regiment, in disgrace for overthrowing one of the governors sent out to stop the rum trade, was recalled to Britain in 1810, and was replaced by more disciplined troops who were barred from trading at all. The government also showed common sense and sent out to the colony British money for use in its internal transactions.

This example illustrates some of the problems with some goods that are chosen to be money. Ideally, money should be durable, which is not the case with goods like rum, or the cigarettes used in prisoner of war camps and some ordinary prisons. Salt, for instance, easily spoils, and is not easy to transport from one place to another except in small quantities that would not buy much. Shells can get broken, slaves can become ill and die, horses wander or are stolen.

Hence, money tends to be either metallic (gold, silver, bronze, brass, nickel, etc.) or specially printed paper carefully engraved to inhibit forgeries. It does not matter too much what number system is used to denominate the currency, as long as it is a constant series be it twelve pence to the shilling, a hundred pence to the pound, a hundred cents to the dollar, or sixteen annas to the rupee.

Money must be easily recognisable by all who trade and use it. This is achieved by the state mint stamping its standard sized and uniformly weighted coins with simple designs, usually with a likeness of the ruler or some other symbol of nationhood. Wherever the coinage circulates it advertises the power and authority of the government that issues and guarantees it.

The currency must be scarce enough to prevent diluting its relative purchasing power, yet not too scarce that other, informal, more easily obtainable forms of money become acceptable. The currency should also be stable in its purchasing power, though the inflationary experience of the last fifty years has undermined this ideal to the extent that inflation has become a major problem for almost all countries and their currencies today.

Money gradually evolved from gold and silver coinage to paper currencies that are 'backed' by the government. Gold, from an early age, has been universally acceptable as a means of trade both within and between countries. Precious metals have always been scarce enough to ensure that their supply does not suddenly disrupt the price system.

A Spanish silver dollar, for example, had a dollar's worth of silver in it, i.e. what it cost to mine and refine the amount of silver in the actual dollar coin. This coin was used for trade all over the commercial world. But, as these economies developed they substituted *token* money for the real thing. Instead of a dollar's worth of silver, carefully weighed and stamped by the government, a paper dollar was issued at a fraction of the production cost of the dollar's worth of output each paper dollar could buy.

Early bank notes were convertible on request into gold or silver at full face value. This ensured their general acceptability and made their use even more common, which was good for the economies concerned as their governments had a problem of funding steady growth in economic activities beyond the ability of gold and silver production to cover the increasing number of transactions. Printing presses can work faster than gold mines, though this brings with it some serious disbenefits when governments print more paper than their country's economic growth requires.

With the growth in token currencies, countries developed banking systems that came to play important roles in their economies. Early banks often issued their own notes, but eventually the issuing of currency became a monopoly of the government's central bank. We shall examine the role of banks in Chapter 20.

Money in its modern form has three main roles. First, it must facilitate trade and exchange; it must, in fact, be recognised by all citizens as the general means of payment for any good or service available in the economy. Money that inhibits trade, perhaps because it is not trusted by the people, or because it has some of the defects mentioned earlier (too bulky, given to wastage, etc.), will eventually cease to be used as money.

Secondly, money must be a measure of purchasing power. It is wanted only because it can be used anywhere in the territory to acquire real goods and services in distinct proportions (or prices).

On knowing the money prices of corn and dates we know the relative worth of corn in terms of dates. If corn is ten dollars a tonne, and dates are five dollars a tonne, we know that corn is worth twice that of dates per tonne.

Thirdly, money must be of durable value, that is, we must be able to save it today and spend it at some time in the future for a similar quantity of real goods and services. If this is not the case, perhaps because of inflation, or a change in coinage following a revolution, people will prefer to hold their future purchasing power in some other form (gold, say). If, on the other hand, you can be sure of its future purchasing power you can be persuaded to hold on to it as your store of value.

The monetary economy is the most common form of economy in the modern world. True, there are populations that still live in subsistence economies, with little use for their country's currency, assuming they could acquire any of it, but the majority of the world's economic activities are carried out through the medium of money. Even the subsistence economies, when they trade with other countries, do so largely in money, though there are a growing number of instances of international barter deals (or 'counter trade' as the United States describes it) being agreed between countries that are short of internationally acceptable forms of money.

Money in the modern industrialised economies is the most common means by which households, businesses and government conduct their many transactions. Billions of dollars worth of business is carried out with money in one form or another (including, as we shall see, cheques drawn on banks), and millions of people are so in the habit of using money that they probably could not conceive of a system that did not use it, and almost certainly, they hardly think about how money works in their daily lives.

Money has long been a 'mystery' to most people; they know they need it, and often go to great lengths to acquire it, but as to what it is, why it was created, and how their living standards depend upon it, they would be hard pressed to answer. The next chapters will, hopefully, continue to unveil that mystery for you!

Chapter 19

As good as gold

IF YOU HEAR SOMEONE TELL YOU that something is 'as good as gold', you know, even if you have never owned any gold, that you are on to a good thing. Why? Because gold has long been one of the most treasured of the precious metals. It is so precious that mass murder has been committed in pursuit of it (consider the destruction of the Aztec civilisation by the seventeenth century Spanish), near hysteria has followed new sources of it (the famous Californian, Alaskan and Australian 'gold rushes' of the nineteenth century), and almost everybody has heard of the awesome warning of the tale of King Midas, whose greed for gold destroyed everything he touched.

Keynes half mocked the passion for gold mining, though he well understood the role that gold has had on the wealth-creating process from its spur to production of other things in order to acquire stocks of it. But the idea of sinking shafts deep into the ground to extract an ore at great expense and risk of life and limb, only to store its smelted extract, gold, in well guarded vaults (often underground!), often strikes me as a mild example of human folly.

Gold played an important part in the evolution of the banking system and through this of the modern system for creating money. The early goldsmiths, who, with great artistic skill, transformed the pure yellow metal into artifacts for those rich enough to adorn their persons or their properties with gold, were an essential step towards a modern monetary system.

Goldsmiths had to have a very secure storage system for their gold stocks in case thieves made off with their treasure. And while they were working their clients' own gold into bracelets or necklaces they had to ensure its safekeeping, for if they were less than careful with the treasures of the rich and powerful (for if you were one you were also the other) they could lose more than their own wealth. Kings and princes were not known, in those years, for their squeamishness when it came to punishing those who roused their notoriously short tempers.

As the countries of Europe grew richer, so the possession of gold spread downwards to the rich merchants and officers of the state. To protect their own gold they could place it with a goldsmith for safekeeping. In return the goldsmith would issue a paper receipt, and, on presentation of the receipt would return the gold to its owner. If a major purchase was made – a landed estate for example – the owner of the gold could redeem his precious metal and use it to pay the owner of the land. In turn, the owner of the land would return the gold to a goldsmith, perhaps the same one used by the purchaser, as goldsmiths were not thick on the ground.

It was clearly advantageous, if only for convenience rather than safety, if the purchaser of the land could simply hand over his receipt, endorsed by his signature to the owner of the land, who could take it to the goldsmith if he wanted the gold immediately, or hold on to the receipt until he needed gold for his own purchases.

Thus, paper circulated, fully backed by gold on deposit at the goldsmiths, among people engaged in trading large sums. As long as goldsmiths were reliable, i.e. not given to running off with other people's gold, their paper could circulate freely with little risk to those holding it. If they had any doubts about the probity of a particular goldsmith they could at any time demand gold on production of the receipt.

In a stable society, goldsmiths were generally reliable, and, therefore, the owners of deposits of gold were unlikely, often for long periods of time, to feel it necessary to require a sight of their gold.

When banks began to operate, they did so, roughly on the same principle as the early goldsmiths – they accepted deposits of gold from the public and issued receipts which were convertible on request by whoever acquired them. They also discovered, perhaps by observation, that it was not necessary to match carefully the amount of gold in their vaults with the amount of 'notes' that they issued to the public.

They could issue notes ('banknotes') to the public in excess of the amount of gold they had available to back the notes if anybody wanted gold instead. The public appeared to be willing to accept banknotes as payment for transactions between themselves, and only rarely found it necessary to call on the bank to meet its promise 'to pay on demand' the face value of the note in gold. If anybody did require immediate payment, the bank could make it in gold out of its stock, relatively secure in the knowledge that this would occur only a few times, and would likely be matched by a deposit in gold from somebody else in due course.

Why did banks engage in this, not too risky, business? Because they found it profitable to do so! If they could issue notes against the gold they had in their vaults, in the form of loans to local businesses or households, they could earn interest on the loans. If they could safely issue more notes that they had stocks of their clients' gold on deposit, they earned additional profits from the loans, or they could purchase government securities which also earned them interest.

The key words above are '*safely* issue more notes', with the emphasis on 'safely'. For there was a small risk that everybody who held their notes could demand payment in gold simultaneously, and as the bank did not have enough gold to cover all of its notes, it would fail, bankrupting not just itself but anybody holding too many of its notes.

When a 'run' starts on a bank, perhaps in a rumour-ridden panic, perhaps in a dangerous situation such as a revolution, civil war, or invasion, and it persists beyond the ability of the bank's reserves to pay out against redeemed notes, it will go bust. And this applies to every bank in the world: all banks issue more notes (or, what today we could call *credit*) than they have the means to meet demands for repayment from people who deposit their savings with them.

How much can a bank lend against its reserves? It took a long time, and many bank failures, to get the safe ratio right, and this ratio is safe only for normal circumstances (war, or any collapse in confidence will bust the banks). Prudence suggests a ratio of reserves to issued notes of about ten per cent. Much lower than this results in worthless paper notes if anything untoward happens; more than this means missed opportunities for profitable lending.

A currency that is backed by the promise to redeem the notes in gold is said to be on the *gold standard*. Many countries were on the gold standard up to the 1920s, but all, in effect, have abandoned gold as the backer of their notes in circulation. Modern countries have found it more convenient to have the central (i.e. government controlled) bank in charge of their national issue of bank notes and coinage – it enables the government to profit from its monopoly – and, instead of gold, they back the currency with the authority of the government. This somewhat fictional device – the government promises to pay the holder of one of its notes the face value of the note – is a logical nonsense, but it works because most people accept the government's notes in full payment for any debt they are owed, and for as long as people accept payment in the government's notes it constitutes money in the real sense.

Government-issued money is made acceptable by the legal requirement for everybody to accept it in full settlement of a debt, or risk the debt being cancelled in law if they don't. If you offer to pay somebody $100 against a debt to them of $100, and they refuse to accept the $100, preferring something else instead, you have the full backing of your government (assuming your national currency is in dollars!) to consider the debt cancelled. In the face of this possibility, your creditors are under enormous pressure, backed by the government's determination to ensure the legitimacy of its currency, without which its general legitimacy would be in question, to find your offer of final settlement in government-printed banknotes acceptable to themselves.

For as long as the public accepts government paper notes, even with their logical nonsense about repayment, then these almost worthless notes – they are certainly worth less than their face value to print – are 'as good as gold' in terms of their nominal purchasing power. They are also transportable, divisible, durable (because they are replaceable on a one-for-one basis with crisp new notes from the government's presses), and usable within the entire territory. This makes them money.

Chapter 20

The creation of money by banks

THERE IS ANOTHER FORM OF MONEY in existence, which is created by the banks, namely cheque or current and deposit accounts, and we shall discuss this form of money in this chapter. The money in circulation, be it in the form of government-printed bank notes or government-minted coinage, is supplemented by money that is created not by the government, though the government keeps a close eye on how much is created, but by the banks in the banking system.

The role of banks as creators of cheque or deposit money is partly a historical leftover from the earlier role of banks as the sole creators of money. Governments attained their monopoly on the issue of currency but left the right to create deposit money with the independent banks, though some banks, such as the Scottish banks, still retain the right to issue their own banknotes in place of government-printed notes, but do so under such heavily circumscribed conditions that in effect Scottish bank notes are more a form of prestigious advertising than anything else.

When you deposit government banknotes in your local bank, you are opening a transaction that is analogous to the depositing of gold with the goldsmiths of earlier centuries. You receive a receipt for your money and an entry is made in your current account (a current account is one against which you can issue cheques for the amount that you have deposited with the bank). You can withdraw your money to pay somebody else for a transaction you have undertaken, and that person can re-deposit the money in his or her account with his or her own bank, which might be the same bank as yours or another one. When you withdraw money, your current account is debited by the amount that you have withdrawn and your trading partner's account is credited with the same amount.

Instead of going through the process of withdrawing banknotes to make a payment to somebody else, you can issue them with a cheque drawable on your account for the amount that you wish to transfer. The cheque is normally acceptable as a means of payment, assuming you are in known good standing, or can demonstrate yourself to be to the satisfaction of the person accepting the cheque. The person accepting the cheque will deposit it in his own bank account and, once it has cleared your bank, he can be credited with the amount you have indicated on your cheque. Your bank reduces your current account by the amount on the cheque when it is presented to them, and pays to the credit of the other person the amount written on your cheque.

In this way, cheques are used to transfer money from one account to another, and in the daily exchange of cheques between a country's individual banks a considerable amount of money will pass to and fro between them. Naturally, to save on the transportation of large sums of notes and coinage between banks, a system of transferring the net amounts only, will operate.

If the cheques drawn on one bank for another bank and vice versa are exactly equal, then no money in the form of notes and coinage need physically move from one bank to another. Book-keeping entries in each bank will suffice. The only money that is transferred is in the form of the cheques that move between banks to notify them of which accounts to debit or credit (and with electronic banking, not even cheques need travel, the electrical signals between each bank's computers will suffice).

This puts banks in the same position as the early goldsmiths. They know that the majority of their clients are not going to present themselves at the counter asking for their money deposits. In the case of time deposit accounts (i.e. those that pay interest and require notice of withdrawal) the bank does not have to meet a demand for payment unless the conditions pertaining to the account are met.

The client who has a time deposit account cannot use it for cheque operations, and must physically present himself at the bank for payment in notes. A current account holder, in contrast, can issue cheques to third parties against his account without going near the bank, and can do so without warning the bank of his intentions. For this instantaneous facility, the bank does not normally pay any interest on a current account, though bank competition might induce banks to do so from time to time.

Banks can, therefore, issue credit in the form of the right of borrowers to draw on cheque accounts in excess of the amount of money deposits that they hold on behalf of their depositors. In this way, the cheques, or rather the amounts entered as credits, constitute money when they are issued in payment by those holding them. In a modern economy, the overwhelming majority of money in the economy is made up of cheques written against accounts held by banks; the rest of the country's money is made up of the notes and coins in public circulation.

If banks account for most of the supply of money in the economy, how does the government control the money supply? We shall illustrate, with a simple example, the way the banking system creates money and then see how the government arranges its monetary policies to control how much money the banks create.

The process is very much like the investment multiplier process that we discussed earlier, at least as far as the arithmetic is concerned. I shall illustrate the process with a simple arithmetical example, involving clients of two of Ogoland's banks, the First National Bank of Ogoland (known

The creation of money by banks · 109

locally as the 'First National') and the Ogoland Merchants' Trust Bank (the 'Merchant Trust'), though it should be noted that the example would not be different in substance if all the transactions occurred with clients of the same bank, or of clients of all the banks of Ogoland.

We can begin with the First National receiving, say, $1,000 as a deposit from one of its clients in the form of Ogoland government banknotes. This is a *liability* as far as the First National is concerned, because it can be demanded by the depositor at any time, but it is also an *asset* for the bank as it adds to its reserves, which are available for repaying any depositor who arrives at the counter demanding cash against his account.

The $1,000 is, however, an excessively high reserve for the First National, operating as it does in a fractional reserve banking system. It is most unlikely that it would be required to pay out all its deposits at the same time, and experience suggests that about 10 per cent is a *safe* reserve to hold against its deposits. In practice, the government might require more than ten per cent to be held by all banks in their reserves (in the UK it is presently 12.5 per cent) but for our illustration let us stick with Ogoland's easier arithmetic of ten per cent.

At ten per cent, the First National can safely lend $900 of the $1,000 deposit to a person who requires money for some approved purpose (approved, that is, by the bank!), and once a borrower has been found, and has spent the $900 (by writing a cheque for that amount to some other person) the bank's reserves fall to $100 out of the original $1,000 deposit. Suppose now that the cheque is paid to somebody with a cheque account at the Merchant Trust, which enters the amount of $900 in that client's account.

Now the Merchant Trust's deposits have risen by $900. It requires to hold only ten per cent of them as reserves, so it can lend $810 (10% × $900 = $90, and $900 - $90 = $810) to a borrower prepared to pay it interest for the loan of $810.

Suppose its borrower draws a cheque for $810 and pays it to a client of the First National. This increases the deposits in the First National by $810, of which only ten per cent is required for safe reserves. The First National loans $729 (10% × $810 = $81, and $810 - $81 = $729), which when drawn upon is deposited by the payee of the cheque in the Merchant Trust, and immediately creates an opportunity for the Merchant Trust to loan 90 per cent of $729 (= $656.10). The process can continue until the money created from the initial deposit of $1,000 equals $9,000 (i.e. $10,000 - $1,000 original deposit), and it is illustrated in Table 4 (see page 102).

Each new deposit is smaller than the previous one because ten per cent of each round is added to the reserves. The sum of all the rounds (not shown in the table because of the messy arithmetic) will be $10,000, suggesting a multiplier of ten, which from your acquaintance with the investment multiplier should not be a surprise: the bank multiplier works on exactly the same basis as the savings multiplier, i.e. the smaller the

TABLE 4: **Deposits created**

Bank	Amount	Reserves	Source
First National	$1,000	100	currency deposit
Merchant Trust	$900	90	cheque from FN's borrower
First National	$810	81	cheque from MT's borrower
Merchant Trust	$729	72.9	cheque from FT's borrower
First National	$656.10	65.6	cheque from MT's borrower
...	...	...	...
...	...	...	...
	$10,000	$1,000	

required reserves/marginal propensity to save, the larger the creation of money/addition to national income.

The sum of all the additions to reserves will be $1,000, or the same as the original deposit, in much the same way as the addition to saving of an original investment will equal the original injection of investment when the savings multiplier has worked itself through the system.

It should be noted that in our simple example we have assumed that the Merchant Trust is prepared to expand its deposits on receipt of cheque payments on behalf of clients and that First National is also prepared to continue expanding its deposits on receipt of cheques from the Merchant Trust. If either bank does not continue to expand its deposit in the way illustrated – and they might have good reason not to do so – the bank multiplier will come to a stop before it has worked through the system. Again this is analagous to the savings multiplier where a recipient of income has a different marginal propensity to consume from that of participants in earlier rounds, or where some of the expenditures are leaked in the form of imports or taxation.

To see how the government controls the banks' profit-seeking propensity to create money we must examine the workings of the country's central bank and its participation in 'open market operations'.

Chapter 21

Open market operations

WHEN THE INDEPENDENT BANKS create money through expanding bank deposits, they increase the money supply by the amount by which they expand their demand deposits. The expansion of the money supply is bound to be a concern of the government for it affects various aspects of economic activity, including the rate of interest, and through this the amount of intended investment and the relative price stability or rate of inflation.

The governments of most countries operate their monetary policies through a central bank (referred to here as 'the Bank'), usually owned by the government, or managed on its behalf and to its instructions, or by statutory guidelines. The Bank of England (actually founded in the seventeenth century by a Scotsman!) is the world's oldest central bank, and carries out monetary policy on behalf of British governments.

While individual countries manage their monetary policies through their own central banks in different ways, most conform more or less to the general outline given in this chapter.

A central bank has three main functions:

First, it acts as a banker to the country's independent banks, by receiving deposits from them, transferring funds between them, and, like for any other client, making loans to them when circumstances force them 'into the Bank';

Secondly, the Bank acts as a banker to the government, by holding government funds in various accounts, permitting government departments to issue cheques against those accounts, and acting as a lender to the government when it needs to raise money for its purposes;

Thirdly, the Bank controls the country's money supply, either by issuing national currency or by means of *open market operations*. It also regulates the activities of the independent banks.

The Bank's role in respect of the independent banks is to be a 'lender of last resort'. A bank, that is otherwise soundly managed, might require access to cash funds to meet an immediate obligation, and the Bank will supply these funds and charge interest on them. By being able to vary the interest rate it charges, or to demand immediate repayment of a previous loan, the Bank can penalise an independent bank for pursuing certain policies that it disapproved of in the current circumstances, or it can encourage it to undertake other policies that it deems to be in the interests of the economy.

The Bank's relations with the independent banks do not stop at being a lender of funds. It can set, and alter, the reserve ratio that it feels is most prudent in current circumstances. By raising, or lowering, the reserve ratio of the independent banks, the Bank can bring about a contraction or expansion (via the bank multiplier) of credit in the economy. If the Bank were to double the reserve ratio from ten per cent to twenty per cent, the independent banks would be constrained from creating deposits for potential borrowers, and this would severely curb economic activities in the country (assuming, of course, that there was untapped economic enterprise searching for bank loans to carry on their businesses).

A less drastic regulator used by the Bank, is that of 'special deposits'. In this case, the Bank requires the independent banks to deposit some proportion of their reserves with it and does not allow them to count these reserves as part of their own reserves against lenders' requests for repayment. Thus, if the Bank tells the First National and the Merchant Trust to deposit $10 million each with it, and the $10 million cannot be counted in their reserves, they would have to constrain their lending to bring it into line with the ten per cent reserve requirement, or risk imprudent lending and, perhaps, serious financial difficulties if loans to them are called for payment.

The Bank can be as heavy handed in its relations with the independent banks as it needs to be to bring about discipline in the creation of money. Usually, hints of disapproval by the Bank are sufficient to constrain the other banks from behaving in a way that the Bank thinks is either reckless or contrary to its government's policies. The Bank's powers to inflict increasingly severe financial pressure on a bank do not need to be applied in most cases, for even a semi-public comment by the Bank about what it thought was wrong with a particular bank's lending policies could endanger public confidence in any bank that was behaving imprudently.

If, however, circumstances warrant speedy action, the Bank can call in loans, impose heavy interest charges on existing loans, and call in reserves as special deposits. No individual bank is likely to be able to withstand this kind of pressure with impunity. In the last resort, the Bank can, in many countries, withdraw an independent bank's licence to act as a bank.

The real power of the Bank in controlling the money supply comes through its conduct of open market operations (OMO), which is basically the selling and purchase of government securities in the open market to banks, financial institutions, pension funds, businesses and to individuals.

A government has two sources of income: taxation and borrowing. Taxation is a compulsory levy on households and businesses. Borrowing from the public requires voluntary action by households and businesses. They are not compelled to lend to the government (at least in democracies) and must be persuaded by competitive interest rates in choosing alternative uses of their money. This has important consequences as we shall see.

Suppose the Bank wishes to reduce the reserves of the independent banks, and through this curtail credit. It does this by offering to sell government *bonds* in the open market, and, if the price is attractive enough, i.e. cheap rather than dear, it will achieve this objective. In exchange for a bond – a printed piece of paper suitably embossed with impressive official language, committing the government to pay interest to the holder – the government receives a cheque from the person who purchases the bond. This cheque is presented by the Bank to the purchaser's own bank and the price of the bond is deducted from the holder's account and transferred to the government's account at the Bank by a reduction in that bank's reserves held there.

The bond holder now has a government security (a sheet of paper) and less money on deposit in the local bank; that bank holds less cash at the Bank and has reduced its reserve ratio by the amount the bond holder spent on the government bond. If its reserve ratio falls below the required legal minimum, the bank will have to restore it or risk the consequences: legal retribution or a run on its resources. It will achieve this by adjusting its lending, such as by contracting fewer loans to the public, calling in some loans that are due and not renewing them, or by selling off some of its other assets (perhaps government securities) to the public, which reduces the purchaser's deposits in the banking system.

Alternatively, suppose the Bank wishes to increase the reserves of the independent banks, and through this expand credit in the economy. It achieves this by offering to buy back from the public previously issued bonds, and, if the price is persuasive, i.e. high enough, it will achieve this objective.

When the seller receives his cheque from the government for the bonds, he will deposit it with his own bank, which, in turn will have its deposits with the Bank increased by that amount. The Bank now has the bond, but less cash equal to the price of the bond; the bondholder's bank now has an increase in its deposits equal to what the government paid for the bond; and it can increase its lending to borrowers by whatever amount preserves its reserve ratio.

Open market operations by the Bank affect the official rate of interest, which in a modern economy is influential in determining the rates of interest across the entire spectrum of lending.

Consider what happens when the government's Bank wants to sell a bond to the public. If you are anxious to sell you cannot be too firm on your price. In other words, to persuade the public to buy the bond the Bank will likely have to lower its price.

Suppose the bond it wishes to sell promises to pay the holder $5 a year and its nominal, face value, price is $100, this means that the interest rate is five per cent, and suppose that in order to sell the bond, the bank's judgement is that it will not be purchased unless it is offered at a price of

$50. Reducing the bond price to $50 has the effect of increasing the rate of interest paid on the bond from five per cent to ten per cent, for a payment of $5 on a loan of $50 is ten per cent.

In other words, a reduction in the price of government bonds increases the rate of interest; and, conversely, a rise in the price of government bonds reduces the rate of interest.

To see this latter effect, consider the situation when the nominal price of bonds is $100 and annual payment is fixed at $5 (equal to five per cent), and suppose that the government wants to buy back its bonds. If you are anxious to buy you will have to raise the price you offer to a potential seller. Now suppose that the Bank's best judgement is that to persuade the public to part with government bonds it will have to offer them $200 per bond. This has the effect of lowering the rate of interest, for whereas a $100 bond got you $5 (or five per cent) interest before the Bank entered the market for bonds, you are now getting only $5 on a $200 bond, or two and a half per cent interest per bond. The rise in the price of bonds has reduced the rate of interest from five per cent to two and a half per cent.

When the Bank engages in open market operations to sell bonds, by reducing their price, it is both securing its objective of reducing the money supply (the cheques paid to it drawn on the independent banks) and by raising the rate of interest it has the effect of curbing borrowing by those put off by the higher interest rates charged on their borrowing.

Remember, leaders of businesses compare the prospective yield on an uncertain investment against the certain yield on lending to a bank, or from purchase of a government bond. If the Bank raises interest rates by selling lower priced bonds, it will influence some, though not all, businesses to curb intended investments (with the effect on economic activity discussed earlier).

In reverse, when the Bank engages in open market activities to buy bonds by raising their price, it increases the money supply (the cheques it pays to former bond holders tempted by the higher price) and reduces the rate of interest, which has the effect of encouraging borrowing by those who compare the prospective yields on uncertain but profitable investment against the certainty of a low rate of interest. This will encourage some businesses to invest if they believe that they have profitable opportunities to do so, and intended investment will rise (with the effect on economic activity discussed earlier).

A government selling bonds generally intends to cause a contractionary effect on the economy; if it does not, it must engage in supplementary moves in the bond market to counter the effects of its operations. Contractionary moves, in the absence of special counteraction by the Bank, are always successful in their objectives. Reductions in the credit base of banks, and increases in interest rates, deter the intentions, and the abilities, of businesses to invest.

When a government buys bonds it promotes expansion (unless it takes specific steps in the bond market to avoid this outcome), but, unlike contractionary intentions which are always fulfilled, expansionary intentions need not be. Banks may be able to lend more as a result of the bond purchases of the government, and the rate of interest may have fallen as a consequence, but it does not follow that business leaders are willing to undertake investments even in the more propitious circumstances of credit availability and lower interest rates. A lot will depend on their mood, their feelings about the future, their expectations and, what Keynes called, their 'animal spirits'.

Nor need households that receive government cheques for their bonds necessarily be willing to go out and spend their money on goods and services and help in this way to stir businesses into moods of optimism. They may have swapped their bonds for cash deposits in their banks as another means of holding their savings, rather than see this switch from bonds to cash as an imperative to increase their consumption.

Government control and manipulation of the supply of money is, so to speak, only one side of the coin. We must now examine its other side, namely the demand for money, and this we shall do in the next chapter.

Chapter 22

The classical quantity theory of money

APART FROM A FEW MISERS, and the honourable band of numismatists (people who collect and study coins), the possession of money is not generally desired for its own sake. We desire to possess money because we desire the goods and services that money can purchase, for, in the main, it is only by offering money that we can make our purchases.

Indeed, it is from its purchasing power that money acquires its value. Your national currency is of value because it can be used to purchase goods and services within your country's borders. A ten quonk note in anywhere but Ogoland is unlikely to be worth much more than the paper it is printed on. To a lesser extent, particular currencies are of value only where they are recognised as legal tender, unless they are *convertible* into the local currency.

If you are in the desert and have with you a million quonks, these are totally useless to you in your desire to purchase water from a passing water carrier if the only thing he will take in exchange for his water is a camel, he having no use for paper currency, and certainly none from a country like Ogoland which he has never even heard of!

The amount of money in a country at any one moment will depend on such influences as the number of people in the country, the value of their wealth in that country's currency units, and the proportion of each individual's wealth that the average person prefers to hold in the form of money. The poorer a country and the larger the extent of subsistence self-sufficiency, the less money the population will require to hold compared with what they will require as they grow richer.

The total economic activity in a country in a period of time will involve the use, and re-use, of money (currency plus cheques). To complete these transactions, households and businesses will require to have money to hand, for without money they cannot undertake transactions. Hence, the need to make transactions, as part of the everyday business life of a country, is a powerful motive for households and businesses having a *demand* for money.

The amount of money that is demanded for transactions purposes will depend upon the value of the transactions – the higher the value of the transactions the higher the amount (in units of value) of money in circulation. At any one time there will be some fraction of the total income of the country that its inhabitants find convenient to keep in the form of money.

One person's expenditure becomes another's income, and in turn that income becomes that person's expenditure. The same dollar note is used in many transactions, and, as it circulates from person to person, it performs the transaction role over and over again. Thus, the transaction demand for money is a fraction of the total value of all transactions. The rate at which currency, in performing its transaction role, turns over is known as the *velocity of circulation*. The faster the velocity the lower the fraction of the total value of all transactions that is required to sustain a given level of transactions; conversely, the slower the velocity, the higher the fraction.

The result of the transactions demand for money is that households and businesses must hold stocks of money (known as *money balances*). You are unlikely to visit another city without carrying with you some money to purchase food, perhaps a room for the night in a hotel, and to pay for any transport that you require. No business can be conducted that does not have a stock of money available to pay for deliveries of inputs and occasional expenses.

When households are paid for their labour services they receive money (cash or a cheque for their bank account), which they can retain for the period between pay days and spend to meet their needs. Over the days before the next pay day they will run down their money balances on the puchase of goods and services. The companies that receive these expenditures will increase their own money balances, either in cash or in the form of credits in their bank accounts.

On average, over the pay period, be it a day, a week, a month or whatever, the total money balances held by both households and businesses will be equal to the period's pay bill for the household's labour services. The more frequent the pay periods, the smaller the fraction of money balances that is held on average, because the closer together are payments and expenditures, the less the requirement to carry money balances.

Compare, for example, the money balances required to be held if households are paid weekly with the balances required if they were paid yearly – in the former case, the household will have, on average, half its weekly pay in its pockets, assuming they spend it at a regular rate throughout the week; in the latter case, on average they will be carrying six months' pay about with them, and will have to carry the twelfth month's pay around for eleven months.

It is at this point that the controversy between the *monetarists* and the *Keynesians* opens up. The former group are associated with what is known as the *quantity theory of money* and the economic policies that follow from this theory, and the latter group (though almost certainly unfair to what Keynes actually believed) are associated with the view that money does not have the influence accorded to it in the quantity theory, and in their economic policies they are hostile, to put it mildly, to the implications of the quantity theory.

To appreciate the simplicity of the quantity theory of money, we can present it in its original form, and elaborate on it later.

The value of all transactions in a time period (say a year) consists of two elements: the value of the transactions, or their prices; and the number of transactions that take place.

You should remember from the discussion on the national income accounts that the value of transactions is greater than the value added measure of the national income (because of double counting), but every transaction that takes place requires the deployment of money in one form or another. In other words, the money used in completing an economy's transactions demands must cover all of the transactions that take place, and, though, normally, a fraction of the total value of transactions, because of the velocity of circulation, it is a real activity and not just an accounting one.

The quantity theory is best known for its definitional identity expressed as:

$$MV = PT$$

where M is the quantity of money, V is velocity of circulation of the money stock, P is the price level, and T is the number of transactions that take place in the given time period (usually thought of as a single year). In this form, the quantity equation is an identity, sometimes referred to as a tautology or truism, for by the way each variable is defined, the lefthand side must equal to the righthand side at all times.

When households and businesses engage in transactions they do so at the current prices of the goods and services being transacted. They pay for these goods and services out of their stocks of money and, in order to complete all the transactions, the money they spend and receive must turn over enough times to cover all the transactions at their current prices.

The righthand side, PT, is not equal to national income because the sum of all transactions includes double counting of intermediate goods and services used to produce final output, while national income consists of final transactions only. The stock of money required to finance all transactions must turn over faster than would be required if all transactions were final.

If the only product produced in a year was a $20 textbook, the national income would be $20; but as the textbook is sold by a publisher to a wholesale book distributor for $10, and then sold to a bookshop for $15 and to the eventual customer for $20, the sum of these prices and transactions is $45, though national income is still only $20. The money stock in this single textbook economy must be sufficient to cover the total number of transactions, and, if the velocity of circulation is two (i.e. each dollar turns over twice per year), it follows that the required money stock must be $45/2 = $22.50.

The quantity theory argues that the demand for money (M_d) is a relatively stable proportion of the value of all transactions in an economy, i.e.

$$M_d = kPT$$

where k is the proportion of PT required to be held for transactions purposes in the form of money. This relates the demand for money, which is a stock, with the value of transactions, which is a flow.

If, as quantity theorists believe, the supply of money (M_s) is a stock determined by the government through the Bank, it follows that there will be equilibrium when:

$$M_d = M_s$$

If, for any reason, the aggregate demand for money is not in equilibrium with the aggregate supply of money, whether in the form of an excess demand for money or an excess supply of money, it is a central tenet of the quantity theory that there will be a consequential adjustment in aggregate demand for goods and services.

If a household has more money than it wishes to hold (excess supply of money) it will spend the surplus on real goods and services until its demand for money is brought into line with its stocks; if, on the other hand, a household has less money than it desires to hold for transactions purposes, it will attempt to increase its money stock by spending less on goods and services.

There is an additional, and recently more relevant prediction from the monetarists, namely, that when an economy is close to full employment any attempt to spend an excess supply of money will force up prices and not output. This occurs because k, the fraction of the value of transactions is believed to be relatively constant, and T cannot change because at full employment there are no opportunities to increase output, and therefore, the number of transactions. This only leaves P, the price level, to change.

Hence, an increase in the money supply provokes an increase in the price level, and, by implication, if there is an increase in the price level (i.e. inflation) it indicates that the money supply is being increased above the transactions demand for money.

Now, because the government of a country is in control of the money supply, the appearance, and the persistence, of inflation suggests that that government is following the *wrong* monetary policy. A government can conquer inflation, on this argument, by reducing the supply of money.

Chapter 23

The theory of natural unemployment

FIRST, WE SHALL TAKE A QUICK CANTER through the classical theory of employment, and then discuss the strengths and weaknesses of modern versions of this theory.

A pure classical model of an economy asserts that there is a natural tendency for wages and prices to fluctuate freely and bring about full employment of resources.

If there are unemployed workers, competition among households for work will reduce the wage rate, and unemployment will be eliminated when all who want to work are employed at wages lower than they were when the unemployment appeared; if, conversely, there is a labour shortage, businesses will raise the wage rate to attract people who previously were unwilling to work at the going wage rate.

If there is unsold output, the price per unit of the output will fall until consumers are found who want to purchase it; if there is a shortage of output, consumers will bid up the price per unit of the goods that they wish to acquire, and the increased prices will encourage suppliers to increase output until the excess demand is satisfied.

In other words, full employment is the natural equilibrium condition of a competitive capitalist economy. If we set aside, for the moment, the obvious question of why unemployment persists in the 1980s, we can see the theoretical ideas that lead some economists to come to this conclusion.

The basic ideas behind the automatic tendency to full employment are sound, if, of course, the assumptions necessary to ensure their operation are sound in themselves, in particular that market forces operate swiftly and without resistance to the clear signals of demand and supply disequilibrium. A model of the demand and supply of labour will suffice to bring out the main ideas.

The demand for labour, it has already been shown, is a derived demand. Employers consider their prospects of selling the output that they can produce by hiring labour services and compare their prospective sales revenues with the costs of hiring those labour services. If the wage rate for hiring labour services is less than the revenue from selling the output produced by that labour, it makes economic sense to hire labour services. If it costs more in money wages to hire labour than the product of that labour can be sold for, it makes sense not to hire the labour.

Classical theory believed that the product of labour services was a diminishing function of the number of workers – each additional labourer added less to output than the previous labourer, known as the doctrine of *marginal productivity* (see *Microeconomics*, by Richard Shone), so it followed therefore that a reduction in the wage rate was required to increase the demand for employment by businesses. In this model, the demand for labour services is negatively related to the wage rate (see Fig. 7(a)).

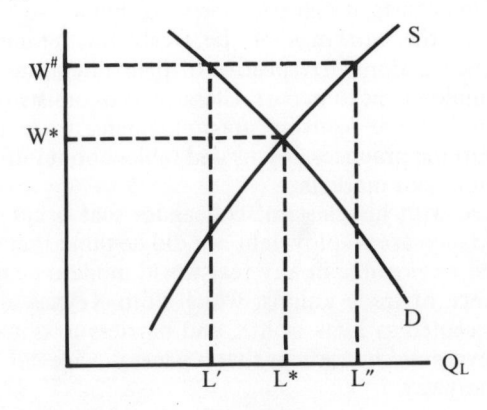

FIG. 7(a): Supply and demand for labour services

From the point of view of households, the supply of labour services was a derivative of the wage rate, i.e. as the wage rate was increased, additional labour services would become available, either from new employees entering the labour market, or from current employees working longer hours.

Households supply labour services in order to acquire purchasing power from their wage earnings. If money wages rise, other things being equal, the purchasing power of households will increase. This purchasing power is the *real wage*, i.e., the goods and services that money wages will buy, and labour services are positively related to a rising real wage rate (see Fig. 7(a)), i.e. a higher real wage induces a greater supply of labour services.

In Fig. 7(a), the demand for labour services by businesses is a downward (negatively) sloped function of the wage rate, while the supply of labour services is an upward (positively) sloped function of the wage rate. Where these two functions intersect we have a situation where the demand for labour is exactly equal to the supply of labour at that wage rate (w^*). Where demand equals supply, we have an equilibrium situation.

In this classical model, the 'cause' of unemployment is quite clear: if the wage rate is higher than w*, at, say, w#, we have a demand for labour services by businesses equal to L', and a supply of labour services by households equal to L".

An excess supply of labour is expressed as unemployment (more people willing to work at the going wage rate than there are employers willing to hire them), and, in the freely competitive classical model, households, faced with unemployment, bid down the wage rate from W# towards W*, cutting unemployment in the process.

If money wages do not fall to clear the surplus of people looking for work, i.e. unemployment persists, it suggests therefore, that non-economic forces are interfering in the workings of the freely fluctuating price system, and, that by their actions, irrespective of their intentions, these forces are causing unemployment to persist. Classical economists include among the non-economic forces causing unemployment: trade unions with their restrictive working practices; myths and fables about individual interests: and inefficient labour markets.

Keynes did not agree with his classical colleagues that a cut in the money wage rate would increase employment nor did he think that such a general wage cut would be possible in any real-world modern economy. Apart from the existence of trade unions, which both Keynes and the classical economists accepted as facts of life, and barriers to downward flexibility in wages, Keynes did not accept that a general wage cut would have the desired effect anyway.

A cut in money wages, i.e. a cut in the actual cash paid out each week to households for labour services, though it was intended to reduce the purchasing power (the real wage) of households, would in fact merely reduce aggregate demand, and through this it would reduce the price level. The net result would be a change in the price level and not a reduction in the purchasing power of the money wage. This would leave the demand for, and supply of, labour where it was, except that a different (lower) set of prices would rule.

Keynes argued, alternatively, that if aggregate demand was stimulated (through, say, the investment multiplier) this would *raise* the price level of output, without necessarily increasing the money wage level, because output will expand but less than proportionately to employment, and, if prices rise with money wages steady, this must reduce the purchasing power of money wages (i.e. reduce the real wage), which will increase the derived demand for labour services, and, through this, reduce unemployment.

It really depended on which way round the stimulus to employment is conceived of as starting: the classical economists thought money wages were flexible downwards, and therefore the stimulus to reducing unemployment should begin in the labour market; Keynes believed that monetary policy was flexible (the government can increase its supply) and therefore the stimulus should begin through government expenditure.

Modern quantity theorists (of which the most prominent has been Professor Milton Friedman in the United States) have continued the classical criticism of Keynesian economics by alluding to an alleged impossibility of securing permanent increases in employment by government-sponsored increases in investment expenditures. If the government attempts to follow Keynes' advice, and increases its expenditures to stimulate employment, it will provoke inflation, and, in some versions of the argument, actually increase unemployment at each level of enhanced government expenditure. In other words, Keynesian demand management is a futile policy that results in higher rates of inflation and growing unemployment.

Friedman began by arguing that there will always be some level of unemployment in an economy (corresponding to *frictional* unemployment as people change jobs, search for new ones, wait for jobs at wage rates for which they believe themselves qualified, etc.) and he calls this the *natural* unemployment rate. Keynes himself always accepted that a fairly high rate of unemployment was a normal feature of an economy – at one time he thought full employment could be defined as including a 3 to 5 per cent unemployment rate to account for this phenomenon. The natural unemployment rate is consistent with equilibrium in the demand and supply of labour at the going wage rate.

To see the significance of Friedman's natural employment rate we must divert slightly to consider the 'Phillips Curve'. Professor Phillips caused something of a sensation in the economics profession (a body of people not wholly given to excitement!) by publishing an article that claimed that there had been an inverse correlation between the unemployment rate and the rate of wage inflation (see Fig. 7(*b*)) in the UK over the period 1861 to 1957.

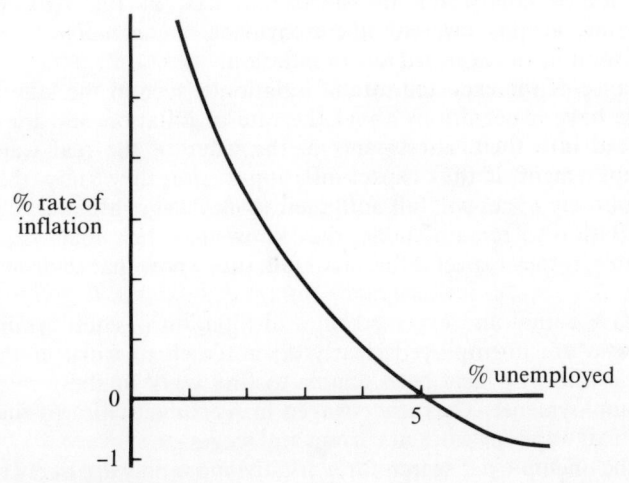

FIG. 7(*b*): **'Phillips Curve'**

The Phillips curve sparked off an entire literature in the professional journals and many research programmes were undertaken all over the world to test its prediction that unemployment and inflation were related in some way.

The implications of the Phillips curve were quickly grasped by policy-makers in governments. The curve suggested that there was a trade-off between the level of unemployment and the rate of inflation; the lower the level of unemployment, the higher the rate of inflation, and vice versa. A government could choose the combination of inflation and unemployment that it thought was tolerable (on whatever mix of economic, social and political considerations were important to it).

Two other features of the Phillips curve are worthy of note: first, at very low levels of unemployment – under 1 per cent – inflation became infinite (hyper-inflation), which would lead to a collapse in the currency, and probably the government with it; and secondly, at higher levels of unemployment, where the curve cuts the horizontal axis in Fig. 7(b), inflation stabilises at around 0 per cent (the 'natural' rate of inflation?) and is not reduced by much more than –1 per cent by additional unemployment.

Ten years after Phillips published his results, Professor Friedman published a critique of them. A year or two later, in the later 1960s, the statistical relationship, so confidently announced between the rates of unemployment and inflation, broke down, and the Phillips curve declined in popularity as an explanation of anything, except the dangers of taking econometrics too seriously.

Friedman's criticism was based on re-asserting classical values about the workings of the market mechanism. The natural rate of unemployment could be thought of as that rate where there is zero inflation, i.e. where the original Phillips curve cuts the horizontal axis in Fig. 7(b). In Friedman's terms, at this level of unemployment, the *actual* rate of inflation is the same as the *expected* rate of inflation.

The significance of the expected rate of inflation is seen in the labour market. People have expectations about the rate of inflation and these expectations feed into their assessments of the value of the real wage offered for employment. If they expect inflation to rise, they know that the real value of their wages will fall until their money wages are raised; if they expect inflation to remain stable, they know that their real wages will remain stable; if they expect inflation to fall, they know that their real wages will rise.

Where we have actual and expected rates of inflation in equilibrium, those people who are unemployed clearly do not wish to work at the going real wage rates, or have been unable to find work at these rates (frictional unemployment). They are engaged in *search* activities to find work at higher real wages or work at current real wages.

The longer the unemployed search for work, the more they are likely to revise their ambitions because there are costs in searching, not the least of which is the difference between their current real income and the real wages of employment. At some point, the costs of job searching and the offer of a job at a real wage lower than the one a person had aspired to will be equal and that particular person will take a job.

It may be that another person, previously working at the going real wage has ambitions to do better, and he will leave his job and engage in search activities. The net result is a regular turnover of people from employment to unemployment and back again, which is simply a form of frictional, or natural, unemployment.

Friedman thought that a trade-off between unemployment and inflation was not possible because the Phillips curve ignores the ability of people to distinguish (eventually) between their money and real wages.

Suppose the government follows the Phillips menu of choice and decides it can accept a higher rate of inflation if the rate of unemployment is lower. In Fig. 7(c), the government decides to go for an unemployment rate of 3 per cent and its associated rate of inflation of 5 per cent and adopts the necessary economic policies to bring this about, perhaps by increasing public expenditure. Presumably it thinks the electorate is more likely to accept a higher rate of inflation than it has experienced so far (assume for the sake of the argument that the economy is sitting where the Phillips curve crosses the horizontal axis, i.e. it has 5 per cent unemployment, 0 per cent inflation), as long as it sees that unemployment has fallen.

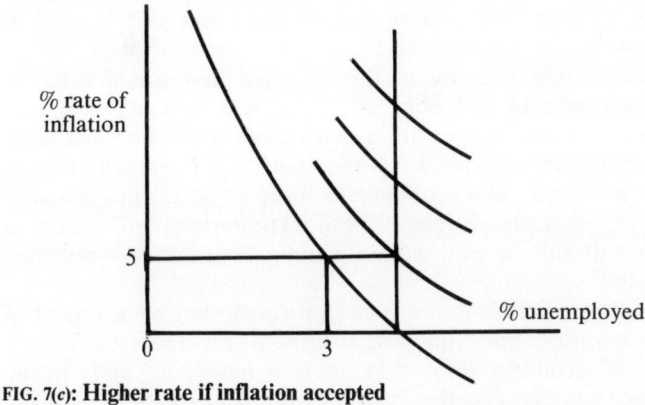

FIG. 7(c): **Higher rate if inflation accepted**

What happens? The rise in public expenditure will reduce unemployment and the rise in employment will increase output and prices. Money wages will rise and people previously unemployed will take the jobs at the new money wage rate. They may believe that their job searches for work at a higher real wage have been justified and be pleased to be back at work. Businesses will hire more workers from households because they will see their sales revenues rising and conclude that effective demand for their products justifies the hiring of additional labour services, and, probably, investment in new capacity as well.

With prices rising, the real wages of employees will not rise in the same proportion as their money wages. In fact, to get the real wage rate we must reduce the money wage by the price rises, for the real wage represents the purchasing power of money. If prices rise and it costs more to purchase the same basket of household goods as before, then the real wage will not have risen at all.

Those households who previously withheld labour services at the previous real wage rate will find themselves back in the same real situation as they were before the government engaged in its manoeuvre to reduce unemployment, and as they become aware of this (assuming they are not macroeconomists who can understand what is happening!), they will reduce their supply of labour services.

Businesses will also discover that the real cost to them of hiring labour services has not fallen relative to the price at which they can sell the additional output the additional employees produce, but that the real cost is the same as before, with money wages rising as fast as sales revenues, and they will be inclined to reduce employment, and cancel or curtail expansion plans. The action of households and businesses as they perceive what has happened will result in a return from 3 per cent to 5 per cent unemployment.

It does not stop here, however. The new equilibrium will not be a return to 0 per cent inflation at 5 per cent unemployment, but a continuation of inflation at the newly created 5 per cent level in spite of the return to 5 per cent unemployment.

Having disturbed the equality of the expected and actual rates of inflation at 0 per cent by inducing an actual rate of 5 per cent, the authorities have created an expectation that inflation will be 5 per cent. Households will expect their wages to anticipate 5 per cent inflation in the next pay negotiations, and businesses will expect their sales revenues to cover a 5 per cent rise in costs. Both expectations will ensure a continuation of inflation, even though unemployment has now returned to its natural rate.

Once inflationary expectations become confirmed, they have a habit of persisting. For example, since inflation at some positive rate has been a feature of the UK economy since 1935, there is hardly anybody in the British workforce who has experienced a period of time when prices have not risen. Inflationary expectations are now, in the 1980s, firmly built in to the attitudes of the British workforce, even with unemployment at over 3 million. The same applies to a greater or lesser degree across all workforces in the world.

This means that when governments attempt to reduce unemployment by Keynesian methods they fail in the long run. All their efforts, though they might lead to temporary reductions in unemployment, result in higher rates of inflation at the natural level of unemployment. In

Friedman's view, this means that the so-called Phillips curve is an illusion; instead of the relationship between inflation and unemployment being negatively sloped, it is, in fact, vertical: for every rise in inflation, unemployment remains stubbornly fixed at its natural level.

More recent evidence of the inflation-unemployment relationship suggests a more complex interaction between them. By adopting monetarist policies (discussed in the next chapter), governments have reduced rates of inflation (sometimes from as high as twenty per cent to under four per cent), but these successes have been accompanied by increasing rates of unemployment (sometimes from below 5 per cent to over 12 per cent). This combination of stagnation and inflation is known as *stagflation* and controversy rages as to what can be done about it.

Chapter 24

Monetarist policies

THE KEYNESIAN CONCENSUS, that dominated the economic policies of most Western governments up to the 1970s, came under sustained criticism with the revival of monetarist ideas. These monetarist criticisms took on a more practical flavour with the election of 'right wing' governments in Germany, the United States and Britain, and the appearance of tendencies to stagflation, i.e. rising and sustained unemployment, in the industrialised countries, accompanied by rising and sustained inflation. Unemployment rates doubled in the early 1970s, while inflation rates went into the middle twenties, particularly following the trebling of the oil price in 1973.

The debate between the mainly fiscal prescriptions of the Keynesians and the mainly monetarist policies of the monetarists is far from over. Much of the debate is also confused with other issues such as the appropriate level of public expenditure, and the degree of competition that should be encouraged in the provision of goods and services. In the UK, for example, 'privatisation' (or, denationalisation) of public utilities and other activities has given the debate a political tone, not all of which is strictly relevant to the economic issues at stake.

A monetarist policy can be pursued by a 'left wing' government, and was successfully applied in the UK under the Labour administration before the Conservatives came to office. It would not be stretching the term monetarist too far to describe the economic policies of the French socialists as monetarist in emphasis, and, in the case of the communist governments of the Soviet Union and Eastern Europe, monetarism is an accepted principle of economic management.

What gives monetarism its popular image of being a 'right wing' solution to economic problems, (or, in extreme reactions to the actions of right wing governments, the belief that monetarism is the supreme economic problem itself!), is its association with free market policies for businesses and the adoption of policies that reduce the growth of public welfare (though not defence) expenditures.

How do monetarists see the macroeconomic problem of the industrialised economies? To answer this in a brief chapter is to risk being too blunt to capture the subtleties of the monetarist position, but as this is an introductory text and not a comprehensive survey I shall accept that risk.

Monetarists lay the blame for persistent and worsening inflation rates on those governments that continue to inject money into the economy in pursuit of the political goal of over-full employment. The monetarist defines full employment as the rate of employment that is consistent with the existence of natural unemployment. This definition ought not to be too controversial as Keynes, as has been noted, appeared to have accepted that 100 per cent employment was not possible, and, indeed, seemed to have accepted that 95 per cent employment was about the best that could be obtained in the actual circumstances of the Western economies.

In the view of monetarists, when a government, irrespective of its political complexion, engages in policies that attempt to drive employment up beyond the natural unemployment rate, it can do so only for as long as it is prepared to accept a rising rate of inflation. If the rate of inflation continues to rise through time, it will bring about a collapse in the currency as people switch out of money into real goods. The experience of hyper-inflation suggests that it leads to political instability (Germany, 1923), though it should be observed that some countries sustained relatively stable political systems for prolonged periods of time even with inflation rates of over 200 per cent (Argentina to 1983, Israel to 1984).

Governments pursue full employment demand management policies for all kinds of reasons, not all of them wicked! Apart from the understandable desire to be re-elected, governments, or rather the people they consist of, do have political philosophies that endorse policies aimed at alleviating poverty, distress and deprivation. To this end they may pursue policies of establishing and expanding welfare provision; they may engage in expenditure on expanding educational opportunities; they may promote universal medical services at no user-cost; they may undertake environmental schemes to improve living conditions, including public house-building; and they may introduce well-staffed counselling services (social workers) to help people cope with of their daily lives.

In sum, a prolonged period of expansion of government expenditure for quite worthy ends could result in an 'over-heating' of the economy as the associated monetary injections drive unemployment below its natural rate.

If, as the monetarists believe, this will result in continuous inflation, and, if, as experience suggests, the result of having continuous inflation is to accept higher levels of unemployment (as foreign competition undermines the private wealth-creating sector by reducing export competitiveness and increasing import penetration) it may be that the economy develops tendencies that worsen the situation on two fronts.

Firstly, it may be that the rising unemployment, in excess of the natural rate, stimulates the very social deprivation that the 'welfare' policies were intended to alleviate, and secondly, the worsening economic performance, that is a consequence of economic failures, may make it more difficult to sustain the government's well intended counter-deprivation policies.

From futile attempts to reduce unemployment below the natural rate, the economy may end up with prolonged periods of unemployment above the natural rate, and with high rates of inflation as well. The monetarist regards this as a situation where the unpleasantness of the 'cure' is better than the unpleasantness of the illness continuing. This last becomes the source of the charges of 'lack of compassion', often targeted on monetarists and politicians who espouse their policies.

A monetarist government would embark on a policy of contracting the *growth* in the money supply. A too sudden reduction in the money supply by draconian means would provoke a drastic cut in national output and probably a great deal of social unrest. Governments that have tried this draconian approach (Chile, for example) have had to support it with harsh, and sometimes violent, suppression of public dissent, suggesting that extreme monetarism on this scale is possible only where military force is available, and where the government is willing to use it (which is probably why monetarism remains unchallenged in the communist countries).

Monetarists in the Western democracies have to accept a longer time table for their policies to work, and indeed, Professor Friedman has *always* advocated a strictly gradual approach, albeit managed with an unbending will. A government determined to slow down, and then reverse, inflation, would announce that from then on the money supply would be increased only at a (low) fixed rate, and come what may it would not be increased beyond that rate no matter how much unemployment might rise above the natural rate. Indeed, the monetarist would argue that if unemployment rises dramatically above what it was while the previous 'Keynesian' policies were in force, this only goes to show the extent to which the wrong policies were pursued under the earlier administration.

The target for a monetarist policy of a gradual reduction in the rate of growth of the money supply and a determined policy of announcing a continuing and steady growth rate, is the inflationary expectations of the population at large. If the government demonstrates its determination to allow only a steady growth in the money supply – perhaps set at a figure close to the real rate of growth in the economy – households and businesses will come to perceive this rate as certain to continue and this will bring their expectations of inflation into line with the actual rate of inflation.

Once this occurs, and is prolonged, the economy will settle down at a state of monetarist full employment, i.e. with natural unemployment only. If the government wants to reduce natural unemployment to some lower figure, it will not set about this by injecting money into the economy in a Keynesian fashion. It will attempt to improve the working of the market economy – more competition for example – to make the participants more responsive to market signals.

The cost of job searching, for example, can be raised by reducing the amount of state-funded unemployment compensation, statutory redundancy pay can be reduced, tax anomalies that discourage searching for work can be eliminated, and information about the labour market improved. If these measures are successful, the time between jobs experienced by significant numbers of the unemployed will be reduced and this will establish a new, lower, natural rate of unemployment.

Whether a monetarist government can 'sell' the very public consequences of its policies to the electorate is not an economic question: charisma, propaganda and political credibility are topics in macropolitics not macroeconomics!

Electorates are not homogeneous entities. They have different interests and gain or lose from a particular economic environment in different measures. Some citizens gain from inflation, particularly those whose incomes depend upon government-funded activities that are paid for by the additional taxes paid under progressive tax regimes from those whose earnings rise in line with the inflation.

Inflation can be popular with a high-spending government. As incomes rise, so does the tax take (a process called *fiscal drag*) and the government ends up with more tax revenues than it would have had in the absence of inflation. This way the government can expand its expenditure without going to the trouble of publicly raising taxes. It can also manipulate tax cuts that cost it nothing, in order to gain electoral popularity, because the tax cuts it concedes represent the tax increases it has generated from inflation in the economy. Those who benefit from the expenditure of inflationary-generated taxes include civil servants who would not otherwise be employed, employees in publicly supported activities which otherwise would not be funded, borrowers of money whose real debt diminishes because of inflation, and people who support the extension of state power.

Other citizens lose from inflation, particularly all those on fixed incomes, or incomes that rise at a slower rate than inflation. This covers pensioners, people on statutory benefits, and people in low income groups whose pay is not negotiated by powerful trade unions. All those who lend money also lose because the real value of the money owed to them is reduced by the rate of inflation. Finally, those who do not support the extension of state power will lose also some psychic satisfaction at seeing their political principles ignored by an inflation-funded government.

In democracies, the decision as to whether a Keynesian fiscal-dominated policy or a monetarist money supply-dominated policy is pursued by the government is not the subject of an academic debate (though academic economists contribute to the debate on each side). The fact that several Western governments have been pursuing avowedly monetarist policies at least provides macroeconomics with a useful empirical test of monetarism, though some monetarists have been very critical of the actual policies carried out by governments otherwise labelled as monetarist – in fact, some monetarists consider that monetarism will get a bad name from the association of *certain* governments with their policies.

But we must always be cautious of judging a macroeconomic policy with an alleged empirical test of it at work. There is no way of knowing whether the economy concerned would have fared better or worse if alternative policies had been pursued. Economics is not a laboratory-based science in which, having tried one set of policies, we can go back to the beginning and try another set in exactly the same conditions. What worked/didn't work in a particular time period may or may not have worked in different circumstances.

Substantial debate is possible on whether Keynesian policies 'worked' in the 1945–73 years; no debate is possible on whether alternative policies would have worked 'better' or 'worse'. Nor can we debate whether Keynesian policies would have worked 'better' or 'worse' in the years since 1973 than the monetarist policies actually pursued by various governments.

We can debate the consequences of certain policies, and whether we prefer this set of consequences to the likely set that might have arisen if alternative policies had been pursued. Whether, however, the consequences we experience are the deliberate result of the policies pursued, or are the unintended consequences resulting from other circumstances that pertain at the time, we cannot be too sure.

If Goliath had had a re-match with the boy David, might he have dodged David's stone? Who knows? We do know that he didn't in the contest he actually had, and, likewise, we can say little more about the periods when Keynesian and monetarist policies were actually tried. Whether this is fair to Goliath, David, Keynes and Friedman is not in our gift to decide.

Chapter 25

Rational expectations

ALL ECONOMIC MODELS incorporate various forms of adjustment by participants to economic signals (prices, queues, excess stocks and so on). The issue that separates the various models of the economy is how, and how fast, the system adjusts. The central problem is that the future is not perfectly known – even the past is imperfectly understood – and alternative models imply different treatments of the phenomenon of expectations.

Consider an imaginary economy in which there is price stability (i.e. no inflation) and where wages are negotiated annually. Employees observe that their output in the past year has risen by 5 per cent (why is not material; it could be due to more efficient organisation, improved machinery, less waste, greater skills, harder effort or whatever). What is likely to be their opening wage claim? We can safely assume that it will be around 5 per cent, for they or their trade union negotiators will aim to attract as much of the improvement in productivity as they can. (The managers will aim to reserve as much of the productivity increase for future investment if they are optimistic of the future, or for price cuts if they are pessimistic, and perhaps look for something for the shareholders too.)

Suppose now the employees read their newspapers and note that the government is to embark on a policy of monetary expansion of the order of 10 per cent (perhaps the previous equilibrium includes unemployment and the government believes that a Phillips type curve operates that enables them to trade off some acceptable inflation for a reduction in some unacceptable unemployment). What will happen?

It would not matter much whether the union negotiators, or the employees, were inclined towards a Keynesian or a monetarist analysis of the economy. If they perceive that there is to be inflation, whether caused by the acceptable trade off of the Phillips relationship, or from the simple arithmetic of the quantity equation, they are likely to include an allowance for the expected rate of inflation in their wage claim. Anybody who does not believe that this would happen has had very little to do with professional trade union negotiators!

Nor will this reaction be confined to the employees. The managers will also anticipate inflation in their assessments of their negotiating position. If they believe that inflation will be greater than 5 per cent, they will know that a concession of a full 5 per cent wage increase will still reduce the company's income in the forthcoming year by 5 per cent (10 per cent inflation minus 5 per cent increase in productivity equals 5 per cent inflation). Employees will know that if they do not get more than 5 per cent, they will suffer a reduction in their real incomes by the shortfall of their increase caused by the change in the inflation rate.

In short, the expectation of inflation will influence their attitude to the share out of the productivity gains. In an economy with stable prices and no increase in productivity, the management and the employees would argue over the extent to which each side's inflationary expectations were to be met, and, all things being equal, the employees would aim to secure a 10 per cent increase in wages to compensate them for the expected 10 per cent inflation. The management would have to pass on the 10 per cent rise in labour costs, plus the 10 per cent rise in the cost of other inputs, in the form of prices. This behaviour, replicated all over the economy, would ensure that prices rose by 10 per cent.

The Keynesian economist, as we have seen, would regard this acceptable if the result was to reduce unemployment by *moving* the economy leftwards up the Phillips curve; the monetarist would argue that the long-term effect would be to *shift* the Phillips curve to the right without any effect on employment beyond the temporary effects of a short term euphoria based on false assessments by employees and companies of the real meaning of the increases in money wages and prices.

A recent extension of the monetarist analysis has been advanced by a number of economists who deny that there would even be a short-term gain in employment – the participants would not have any false impressions of what was happening; they would not misread the rise in money wages as a rise in real wages or a rise in prices as an increase in demand for the company's products. In practice, according to the theory of *rational expectations*, participants would include in their behaviour an allowance for what they expect to happen which will totally negate the intentions of the government.

The government is, in fact, powerless to move employment above the natural level, not just in the long term, as the monetarists argue, but also in the short term too. Any attempt by the government to increase the money supply beyond the rate of increase of productivity, will be pre-empted by the anticipatory behaviour of the participants: employees will raise their money wage demands, and employers will raise their prices, to cover themselves for expected inflation.

This means that the government cannot influence real variables such as employment, output, real wages, and real interest rates. It can only stoke inflationary tendencies – the Phillips curve is vertical in the short and the long run. The only way that the government could influence real events is to conceal what it is up to, i.e. it could mislead the media and announce a ten per cent rise in the money supply while in fact increasing it by twenty or thirty per cent. This way, due to delays in spotting what is going on, it might be able to make some short-term gains in employment, because employees and firms would underestimate the inflationary consequences and adjust their wage and price demands by too little. In democracies at least, such a policy would eventually become public knowledge, adjustments will take place quickly to the higher than anticipated inflation, perhaps with a margin in case the government is still lying, and, in due course, political retribution would follow.

The behaviour of participants who operate under one or other system of expectations can vary enormously, and various economic theories have tried to incorporate expectations in their analyses of what they believe happens in the real world. Keynes certainly thought that expectations about the future course of events were important for any model of the economy. He tried to introduce an approach to expectations that he thought was lacking in the classical models which seemed to imply participants had only static expectations about the future.

Keynes argued that 'animal spirits' – the competitive urge to win – consisted of a speculator taking risks that he could guess better than the market about what was likely to happen to interest rates. By selling when the market was buying, and buying when the market was selling, just before the market realised that it should be doing the opposite to its average inclinations, the risk taker would make large profits, whereas those that followed the market would not.

A dynamic model of expectations would include in it an ability to learn from events and to correct for them in future expectations. People are not immune to experience; if they realise that they have made a mistake they will alter their behaviour, perhaps over-compensating in the process. If they expect inflation to be at five per cent and it reaches ten per cent, they will adjust their expectations to at least ten per cent, and probably, even more.

In the theory of rational expectations, participants do not rely on the past alone to guide their future actions. They sensibly assess the future on the basis of what they know (which may not mean that they are well informed) and will act accordingly, as if they were well informed, i.e. they will react rationally. This leads people to make adjustments that are more or less efficient. Such is the plethora of information available in a modern multi-media society, that people can acquire, at very low, even zero, cost, information about pending events that will be reflected in their expectations. The public is not stupid, even though it might be ignorant. Experience teaches people, and, whatever errors they make individually, overall the errors are minimised and people adjust to their perceptions of the future as if they were well informed.

Thus, without knowledge of economics, or indeed of the quantity theory of money, the theory of rational expectations requires that people will react rationally to whatever information they have and, which, in doing so, will produce behaviour that is not much different from the behaviour we would expect them to engage in if they were fully informed.

If the money supply rises, a rational person, whether he knows of this fact or not, will react to the consequences of that increase – rising prices – as if he were fully informed of the most appropriate behaviour for him in these circumstances. People will include inflation in their wage and pricing decisions because they observe that price rises beget price rises and if they behave differently they will suffer a real reduction in their incomes. They do this with the same confidence that they learn to take a raincoat with them if they see dark clouds overhead when they leave for work in the morning.

In this very brief introduction to the rational expectations theory we do not have space to develop all its implications for macroeconomic policy other than to sketch its broad outlines. It is important because it is a theoretical justification for major policy shifts by several governments (including that of avoiding intervention in certain economic situations altogether).

Among the main assertions of a rational expectations model of the economy we could include the following:

1. people are not stupid when faced with economic signals, if only because these signals are far more blatantly obvious to ordinary people than many economists allow (most people do not suffer from illusions about inflation);
2. a rising price level causes rational adjustments to it by employees (higher money wage demands) and companies (higher prices of own output), and these adjustments are so immediate in their effects that there is hardly any lag at all;
3. because it is rational for people to behave this way, it means that government-inspired attempts at monetary or fiscal policy to increase employment are bound to fail before they begin (if announced, because people will be aware of their inflationary implications), and will fail very quickly if they are carried out surreptitiously (because price rises will show what is happening);
4. in fact, all macro policy is useless because it cannot affect real variables (output, employment, etc.), and can only increase inflation for no gains (even temporary ones) in employment;
5. faced with the impossibility of macro management of the economy, the government can reduce the natural rate of unemployment only by intervention in micro markets, preferably by increasing competition, reducing subsidies, and abolishing restrictive and monopolistic practices.

Criticism of the rational expectations theory is by no means muted. Apart from those economists who hotly dispute the conclusion that macroeconomic policy is irrelevant where it is not destabilising, there are economists, usually of a monetarist persuasion, who doubt whether the instant adjustment process implicit in the theory is a realistic description of what actully happens, even assuming that people behave in a rational manner.

Labour markets are by no means characterised by freely flexible wages or movements of people in geographic space. It may not appear to be entirely rational for an unemployed labourer to remain unemployed rather than offer his services at a lower wage than that which other employed workers are currently earning. But is this so, given the social pressure on people not to auction their services in this way?

Do prices adjust quickly to changes in demand? Time-specific contracts make it difficult to adjust quickly. The motivation for engaging in a long-term contract – security – is just as rational as leaving oneself free to take advantage of changing conditions (though this exposes oneself to disadvantageous changes in conditions). Arbitrage (see page 96, above), while a feature of money markets is not a feature of labour markets. A differential in wages in one occupation does not lead to a speedy drift of employees towards that occupation, nor do entrepreneurs 'store' unused labour with a view to placing it if the market turns upwards.

In sum, while the rational expectations theory has highlighted features of the workings of participants in an economy that have been neglected in other theories, in so far as it rests on a speedy flexible prices and wages system, it must be judged to be deficient in explanatory power regarding the working of actual economies. It provides a rationale to a government for not intervening at one level (macroeconomic) while suggesting it should intervene at another (microeconomic). This alone will insure that rational expectations will remain a feature of economics courses for the foreseeable future.

Chapter 26   PART IV

International trade

THE CASE FOR INTERNATIONAL FREE TRADE is an extension of the case for trade itself between two neighbours. Specialisation raises productivity and output above levels obtainable by general self sufficiency, and the surpluses generated by specialisation are available for exchange, so raising living standards for both parties who trade. If anything is to qualify for a basic truth in economics, this view of trade must be a hot favourite.

The principle of exchange rests on the diversity of resources, talents, opportunities, capabilities, expertise, intuition and motivation of people, even those within the same country, or region.

The division of labour was, perhaps, initiated by an earlier division of roles between the sexes, where women exercised talents as child rearers and men those talents dependent on the use of physical strength (though this assumes that all women are suited for child rearing and all men for activities that require physical effort, which, as any feminist will remind you, is a challengeable assumption).

Whatever the cause, and arguments about it are properly a subject of social anthropology rather than economics, it appears that a division of labour occurred in which some men excelled at hunting, others at building, some at growing, some at saying prayers, and some were confined to being the proverbial hewers of wood and drawers of water.

The division of labour, however it was caused and whoever suffered individually as a result of it, remains one of the great discoveries of human society. It contributed to the survival and enhancement of all those societies that adopted it, whether by original and independent discovery or by imitation. It enabled societies to raise their living standards above the abysmal levels that were (and still are) common to societies that rely on a sexual division alone (the men hunting and gathering, the women child rearing and sometimes gathering).

If a modern society, be it ever so large, confines itself exclusively to producing everything on a self sufficiency basis, known as *autarky*, it will be without doubt poorer as a result.

One of the great divisions in the world during most of this century has been between the socialist states, led by the Soviet Union, and the capitalist states, led by the United States.

For ideological reasons, the Soviet state avoided open trade with the capitalist countries, except for specific products and under highly controlled terms. This has undoubtedly contributed to the Soviet Union's relatively poorer performance compared with the capitalist West, and, now that it could undoubtedly benefit enormously from open trade, it finds this inhibited on the West's part by the latter's concern that open trade would indirectly assist the Soviet Union to grow stronger militarily, and it is inhibited on its own part by the belief that open trade with the West would make the Soviet Union unacceptably dependent on its capitalist 'enemies'.

If this antagonism could be resolved – the suspicion of the Soviet Union about trading with capitalists and the fears of the West about Soviet military intentions – there is no doubt that it would be mutually beneficial for both blocs to increase their trade substantially.

Trade can be based on absolute differences in a country's physical or natural endowments (for example, some countries have oil, others do not) which effectively forces countries to trade for the goods that nature, in its niggardly way, left them without. Trade can also be based on the absolute costs of producing similar goods (one country can produce certain goods at lower cost than can another country), making it worthwhile for higher cost producers to trade with them.

In combination, the absolute differences between two countries, caused by their natural endowments, including climatic differences, and differences caused by the absolute costs of doing similar things in different countries, produce a rationale for specialisation between countries in certain products.

Adam Smith recognised this in the eighteenth century, as I mentioned earlier in this book, when he argued that it would not be sensible for Scotland to produce claret when it could perfectly easily import it from France in exchange for Scottish products that the French themselves did not produce locally. This precept remained true even if the technology, such as glass houses and special winter heating arrangements, could be made available.

For Scotland to invest the considerable capital sums that would be required to create a domestic claret industry (which given Scotland's climate would be an expensive enterprise indeed) instead of investing its scarce capital in activities more suited to its geography, would, in Smith's view, be a monumental waste of its productive assets. By refraining from expenditure in activity that could more cheaply be bought from other countries, Scotland would be able to invest its scarce resources in special activities more suited to its situation. As a result, Scotland would grow richer faster, which, after all was Smith's main concern when he wrote the *Wealth of Nations*.

Instead of using up precious capital in producing importables (things that can be imported from abroad) at greater expense than they can be imported, a country is better advised to invest in exportables (things that can be exported abroad) at lower prices than foreigners can make them themselves. From the resultant trade of its exportables for foreign importables, a country would refrain from wasting its own capital, which could be put to better uses, on expensively manufacturing available and cheaper importables.

Similar reasoning explains why Europe imports bananas from the Caribbean rather than growing them in specially protected greenhouses; why Japan imports coal from Australia instead of investing in alternative and expensive energy sources; why Egypt imports meat from New Zealand instead of diverting scarce capital in agribusiness ventures that are bound to be more expensive than it is to import lamb; and why people in colder climates go to warmer climates for their holidays instead of using the services of expensive sun-ray lamps.

There was and is a case for a country developing its own version of an importable product if, and only if, the alternative is to become vulnerably dependent on a foreign supplier. This is particularly true in the case of certain goods such as defence products, though the 'national security' argument has been used to justify a wide diversity of goods totally unconnected with what we normally associate with defence.

For example, in the early nineteenth century a debate took place in the United Kingdom about the efficacy of importing foreign food, which was considerably cheaper per ton, than domestically produced food. The issue was so intensely fought that several governments were forced into resignation by the depth of feeling about leaving Britain exposed to foreign sanctions.

The lobby for maintaining a monopoly for a domestic food industry referred constantly to the threat to survival if the United Kingdom were to become dependent on foreigners for its basic food supplies. The implication was clear: if Britain was dependent on foreign food supplies, even though they were cheaper to import than to produce domestically, it could become a hostage to the first foreign power that could, by withholding desperately needed food, threaten starvation for its people if it refused to surrender its sovereignty.

In fact the vast prairies of the United States and Canada were ready and able to supply cheaper grain, and later in the nineteenth century, through the development of refrigeration technology, the lamb and beef producers of Argentina, Australia and New Zealand could easily feed the entire population of the United Kingdom with meat at a price per unit substantially below what domestic farmers could ever hope to reach. But this was, in the view of the advocates of the national security argument, an insufficient case for taking the risks that import dependency implied.

In the event, however, the free trade lobby won the day, and Britain gradually increased its dependence on foreign food imports, which were paid for by Britain's exports of manufactured goods to the rest of the world. The decision was made to switch, despite the risks that were well rehearsed during and after the Napoleonic wars of 1783–1815 (and again in the First World War of 1914–18 and the Second World War of

1939–45), from self-sufficiency in food to dependence on others, and to rely on a domestic manufacturing base – the 'workshop of the world' as Britain became known as in the latter half of the nineteenth century. This was, in retrospect, a correct and necessary decision which, if it had not boldly been taken in the 1840s (after much heart searching), would have meant a much slower economic development of the United Kingdom.

The argument about the crucial importance of domestic food supplies to national security has re-surfaced in the modern European Economic Community in its prolonged debates about the rationale for its internal agricultural policies.

The aim of self sufficiency in food production – grossly exceeded in massive surpluses in some products, such as the butter 'mountains' and wine 'lakes' – is often justified by EEC experts on the grounds that self sufficiency in food, no matter what the cost to European taxpayers and the cost in foregone sales by foreign farmers (many of whom are driven into poverty as a result), is ultimately justified by the threat of world famine at some, undated, time in the future.

The national security argument for sustaining, or developing, industries to produce products that can be more cheaply supplied from abroad has to be decided on a case by case basis.

Undoubtedly, there are acceptable national security arguments for ignoring purely economic considerations. Many developing countries, for example, have been investing in indigenous arms industries in order to avoid dependency on unreliable suppliers when their national interests are at stake. If an invasion succeeds because a foreign supplier refuses to send spare parts for the defending armed forces it would hardly be regarded as a benefit of specialisation that the government exposed the country to such risks just because economic theory suggested that it is better in the long run to do so.

However, Adam Smith's point remains valid in the case of a domestic Scottish claret industry – claret, by no stretch of the imagination, could ever be described as an industry essential to national security!

In the main, and broadly speaking (and ignoring genuine national security considerations), there is no worthwhile economic case for producing goods domestically that can be more cheaply produced abroad. The problem of persuading the employees and owners of a declining domestic industry of the economic facts of life when they are facing a damaging challenge from imports, is a most difficult one, thankfully left to politicians and not to economists. The economic case, however, is clear, but it is muddied by the imperatives of short-term political survival.

The temptation to resist the inevitable only prolongs the waste of resources. Switching these resources – people and capital – into new, domestically sound and growing industries, is by far the best solution in the medium and long term.

Specialisation enables a country to take advantage of its natural, or acquired, advantages. Among the latter we include the nurtured abilities of its people, the technological specialities that it develops or inherits, and the unique circumstances for gain that it perceives. Specialising in what it is best at, and foregoing those activities which others can do better, is by far its best economic strategy. Economics is sometimes like sour medicine: knowing how good eventually it will do you does not make its immediate taste any sweeter.

The case for trade when a country has an absolute advantage over its rivals is in theory unchallengeable. It is in its interest to trade those specialities which it excels in for those goods in which others excel.

If, sometimes, a country misjudges its best interests, and goes on producing things it could import much more cheaply, economic theory shows it would be poorer as a result. If a country is determined to ignore the clear economic advantages of specialisation, perhaps under the persuasion of national security, it is, of course, entitled to do so, though such action has an economic cost which cannot be avoided, no matter what the rationale invoked to justify such behaviour. On this point economists have long been unanimous.

But it was the discovery that it was still worthwhile to trade, even when one country could produce *everything* at lower cost than another country, that marked an immensely important intellectual achievement for the economists concerned, and also, incidentally, represents a similar intellectual achievement for today's students when they confront the concept for the first time.

Chapter 27

Comparative advantage

THERE ARE SOME PRINCIPLES OF ECONOMICS that have lasted a long time in the literature, and among these we give pride of place to the early notions as to why trade between countries was to their mutual benefit even when one country had an absolute advantage over others in all of the tradable products. The theory that explained this proposition is known as the theory of *comparative advantage*, and it has been a part of economics teaching for about 160 years. While much of modern theory has refined, where it has not rewritten, the early trade theory of economics, nevertheless, the theory of comparative advantage continues to be included in the first introduction to modern trade theory that most students come across.

That which endures must have something to commend it, and with comparative advantage we find that its simple straightforward notions about the benefits from trade have commendable aspects, not the least that they highlight the fallacies and fictions of those who try to persuade governments (all too frequently with success I am sorry to note) to adopt the destructive policies of protection through import restrictions.

How can it be that it is worthwhile for a country to trade when it can produce everything it wants at a lower cost than a country that wants to trade with it?

The key lies in the difference between absolute and relative efficiencies. A country that is absolutely more efficient than another may nevertheless still be relatively less efficient in producing certain goods.

Consider the case of a textbook author who is competent at authorship and at typing. Suppose that, in fact, compared with the office typist he is better than she is at preparing accurate manuscripts. In other words he has an absolute advantage over her in both authorship and typing.

Should he share his time between writing books and then typing them ready for press, or should he concentrate solely on writing and hire a secretary to type the manuscripts? Even though he has an absolute advantage in both activities, the secretary may have a comparative advantage in typing because, though she has a relative disadvantage compared with the author in creative writing, her relative disadvantage compared with him in typing may be much less.

Suppose the author is much better at authorship than she is, but only marginally better than her at typing. In these circumstances it pays the author to concentrate on the activity he is best at (i.e. creative writing), and not use up his time to do typing when he can hire someone else to use her time to do his typing for him.

The principle of comparative advantage was first applied to trade policy by David Ricardo, an English economist, who combined careers as a financier with that of being a Member of Parliament. His money-making career gave him the necessary financial independence to be absolutely politically independent in parliament (a phenomenon then as now in politics), and he used his parliamentary position in the House of Commons to enunciate economic policies that were based on his method of abstract rigorous reasoning.

I shall illustrate the application of the principles of comparative advantage by considering the prospects for trade between two countries. It is necessary, of course, to make some simplifying assumptions in order to illustrate the points clearly, but though I may alter the facts to suit the example, the central points will apply to any two countries in the real world.

Suppose first that both countries produce only two products, potatoes or cars. We exclude from consideration the probability that each country also produces many more than two products, but to consider more than two products in an elementary exposition of trade theory would unnecessarily complicate the analysis at the price of the clarity we seek.

Now for the sake of clarity in my exposition I will refer to one country as Spain and the other as Egypt. It is always more interesting to give examples using real world names, rather than referring to them as *A* and *B*, though by doing so I run the risk of causing offence where none is intended. Hence, let me say that what follows is not a description of the actual situations in either country nor of their prospects for the future.

To suggest that Spain is better off producing cars rather than potatoes is not to say that Egypt is forever condemned to producing potatoes rather than cars. Egypt, as is well known, already produces many advanced industrial products, including helicopters, jet aircraft and modern tanks. It is one of the most industrialised of all the Arab states, and it already competes with Spain in agricultural produce. In short, my example, while not descriptive of the actual relationship, is at least plausibly realistic.

Suppose now that because Spain has a larger GNP than Egypt it can produce more of either good (potatoes or cars) than Egypt; Spain can use all its productive resources to produce, say, 3 million tonnes of potatoes *or* 600,000 cars, while Egypt, using all its productive resources, can produce 2 million tonnes of potatoes *or* 100,000 cars.

On the basis of these fictitious figures, the theory of comparative advantage tells us that Egypt has a comparative advantage in potato production over Spain, even though Spain has an absolute advantage over Egypt in both products. How so?

We can see this by considering the opportunity cost of each product for each country. Suppose, for example, that Egypt decides it wants to divert some of it productive resources into producing more potatoes, say an extra million tonnes. Egypt knows that to do this will cost it 50,000 cars in lost production because if it re-allocated its productive resources to increase potato output by a million tonnes it must forego the use of these resources in car production. This is so because it can use its resources to produce one *or* the other product only and the same resources cannot be used twice – its productive resources can produce *either* a million tonnes of potatoes *or* 50,000 cars.

This statement tells you the *opportunity cost* to Egypt of producing potatoes as opposed to producing cars.

Now in the case of Spain, similar reasoning about opportunity cost applies. If Spain decided to produce more potatoes, say, an extra million tonnes, it would cost it 200,000 cars in foregone output. Why? Because Spain can produce either 3 million tonnes of potatoes or 600,000 cars, and assuming that the same ratio applies for any smaller quantities (as we do), it follows that the opportunity cost to Spain of using its resources to produce potatoes instead of using these resources for car production is in the ratio of 1 million tonnes potatoes to 200,000 cars.

Clearly, in producing potatoes instead of cars, Egypt has a comparative advantage over Spain even though Spain has an absolute advantage in both products – Egypt is compelled to give up less cars than Spain per million tonnes of potatoes, or, to be precise, 50,000 cars for every million tonnes of potatoes in Egypt, compared with 200,000 cars for every million tonnes of potatoes in Spain.

Spain, however, has a comparative (and absolute) advantage over Egypt in the production of cars. It costs Spain 500,000 tonnes of potatoes (in foregone output) if it uses its resources to produce 100,000 cars, while in Egypt it would cost two million tonnes of potatoes (in foregone output) if it was to produce that amount of cars.

Spain, being a richer country, can out-perform Egypt in the absence of trade in both products and, without trade, will have to produce some combination of both potatoes and cars, assuming, as we do, that its citizens wish to consume both cars and potatoes.

To see what benefits trade can bring to each country in the situation described above we can suppose that each economy starts off with a given combination of cars and potatoes in production. Suppose, say, we have Spain producing, 1,500,000 tonnes of potatoes *and* 300,000 cars, while Egypt, on the other other hand, is producing, say, 1,000,000 tonnes of potatoes and 50,000 cars.

Can both countries improve on their consumption of potatoes and cars? Yes! If, that is, each country specialises in the product in which it has a comparative advantage, it can increase output in that product and exchange some of it for the good that the other country produces.

This requires that Spain reduces its production of potatoes and diverts those productive resources that are released by this action into car production. On the arithmetical ratios mentioned above, Spain could increase its output of cars by 100,000 to 400,000 and in doing so it would reduce its output of potatoes from 1,500,000 tonnes to 1 million tonnes (because, remember, the opportunity cost of 1 million tonnes of potatoes in Spain is 200,000 cars, therefore 100,000 cars costs it 500,000 tonnes of potatoes).

Egypt could make a similar decision to rellocate its productive resources between car and potato production. It could, for example, cease car production altogether, and use the productive resources that this drastic step releases to increase potato production from a million to two million tonnes.

Egypt and Spain could then open trade with each other. Egypt could ship a million tonnes of potatoes to Spain in exchange for 100,000 cars. This gives Egypt its original pre-trade consumption total of a million tonnes of its own potatoes (it produced 2 million tonnes, shipped one million tonnes, and has a million tonnes left) plus, now, as a result of trade, an extra 50,000 cars over the 50,000 it produced when its domestic output consisted of both potatoes and cars. Egypt must be better off than it was before as a result of its trade with Spain.

What can be said about Spain's post-trade position? It has also benefited. It has 300,000 cars for domestic production, having produced 400,000 and exported 100,000 for the million tonnes of potatoes from Egypt. In the case of car consumption, Spain is no worse off than before switching domestic production for the purposes of trade, but as it now has 2 million tonnes of potatoes for domestic consumption instead of 1,500,000 before trade it must also be better off. In fact, by sacrificing 500,000 tonnes of domestic output of potatoes, switching the resources into producing an extra 100,000 cars and exporting them to Egypt for a million tonnes of potatoes, it is better off by 500,000 tonnes of imported potatoes. Egypt, by comparison is 50,000 cars better off. Both have gained from trade.

I have summarised all these transactions in Table 5.

It is a fair question to ask: with the case, from the consumers' point of view, so cleary in favour of free trade, why do countries the world over impose restrictions on trade? Because, the realistic answer would run, as with most things in life, there are gainers and losers when any change is proposed from one situation to another.

Governments, unfortunately in my view, often listen to the lobbying of minority interest groups, or can be frightened of the electoral consequences of not paying heed to their demands, and in consequence they impose tariff barriers, quotas and other restrictions in response to the cries for help (i.e. protection) from one of the most powerful interest groups in any country, namely, its producers.

In our example, Egypt dismantles its car industry, or, more relevantly, for the time being it has forgone creating one, preferring to concentrate its resources in the activity in which it has a comparative advantage:

TABLE 5: **Benefits from trade**

---

1. *Absolute advantage of Spain:*
   If Spain and Egypt produce either potatoes or cars:

   Spain: 3 million tonnes of potatoes *or* 600,000 cars
   Egypt: 2 million tonnes of potatoes *or* 100,000 cars

2. *Production and consumption without trade*
   If Spain and Egypt produce both potatoes and cars:

   Spain: 1,500,000 tonnes of potatoes *and* 300,000 cars
   Egypt: 1 million tonnes of potatoes *and* 50,000 cars

3. *Production with trade*
   If Spain and Egypt produce according to comparative advantage:

   Spain: 1 million tonnes of potatoes and 400,000 cars
   Egypt: 2 million tonnes of potatoes and no cars

4. *Consumption after trade*
   If Spain and Egypt exchange 100,000 cars for 1 million tonnes of potatoes:

   Spain: 2 million tonnes of potatoes and 300,000 cars
   Egypt: 1 million tonnes of potatoes and 100,000 cars

5. *Increase in consumption after trade*
   Spain: 500,000 tonnes of potatoes; Egypt: 50,000 cars

---

potato production. In due course Egypt's productive abilities might induce it to start car production, as it has already done in certain advanced military products.

Comparative advantage does not freeze a country into its first choice in specialisation. Relative productivities do change through time and what is non-viable in one decade, given the capital stock and technological experience of a country, may become viable in a subsequent decade, providing it can increase its capital stock and improve the productivity of its workforce.

Economic growth is one route to a widening of a country's domestic production options. Ironically, embarking on protectionism, when a currently operating domestic industry is under threat from imports, is one sure way to freeze a country's productive options and delay the necessary adjustment of its productive resources to alternative opportunities. Accepting the imperatives of comparative advantage makes a country more adaptable to change, and therefore to growth, than the reactionary, though understandable, policies of protectionism.

We can see the basis of demands for protectionism by considering the adjustments that are required in the context of the model developed above. The decision of the Egyptians, for example, to concentrate on potatoes might be good news for those employed in the potato business but is not so hot for their fellow citizens, formerly in the Egyptian car industry. Egyptian car workers will lose their jobs, and, in the simple two-products model above, if they want to work, they will have to become potato workers or they will become unemployed.

Even in Spain, potato production will fall by 500,000 tonnes and this will cause unemployment among Spanish potato workers. Car production will increase by 100,000 units and this will increase employment in the Spanish car industry. But you can bet your last kilo of potatoes to a car that the losers – those who have to change or do without jobs in both Egypt and Spain – will be none too happy about the consequences of trade between their two countries, even though, as consumers they are clearly going to be better off, because in both countries they have no less of one product and much more of the other to consume, without, it must be stressed, any diminution in the quality of the goods being traded.

We know this last point because if foreign goods are of lower quality, and are more expensive, than domestically produced goods there is no need for protection from them. Consumers can be relied upon to discriminate in favour of quality and lower prices. Therefore, we conclude that demands for protection are demands for special treatment, and *always* (there are *no* exceptions!) involve attempts to force domestic consumers to buy more expensive domestic produce in place of cheaper (and, often, better quality) foreign produce.

Not that the demands for protection are dressed up in this frank way. Almost always, their sponsors imply that the national interest is at stake, it being more acceptable to cloak one's personal interests in an outburst of patriotism.

Protection will be demanded to allow 'fair competition' against the 'low wages' of the Third World, though, when competition from high wage countries like Germany threatens cosy domestic businesses, the case for protection has to change its arguments if gullible government ministers and trade union leaders are to take it seriously.

The scope for protectionist arguments is almost unlimited. The producers concerned can make out that it is a matter of protecting 'infant industries' – if the industry is new – and 'declining or senile industries' if the industry is old. For those mid-life industries in-between, the case for protection can be made on 'security of supplies or technology' grounds, or the need to 'maintain domestic employment in depressed regions', or, failing all else, 'temporary arrangements to allow the industry to adjust to the new challenges of mid-life'!

The fact remains that demands for protection always work against the interests of consumers (all of us) in favour of the demand of producers (some of us). The theory of comparative advantage establishes the case for free trade and the fact that it is still around after 160 years suggests its detractors have been unable to dislodge its compelling logic, even if they have been successful from time to time in persuading governments to adopt protectionist policies that make their own citizens worse off than they need to be.

Chapter 28

Foreign exchange rates

DESPITE THE EXISTENCE OF TARIFFS and other barriers to trade, there is no doubt that international trade is a major influence on all economies. It brings with it a number of problems, which form an important part of a government's management of the domestic economy, and properly secures a place in any macroeconomics textbook.

The immediate and obvious problem with international trade is that exporters have to be paid in their own country's currency, unless trade takes place under barter conditions, which, as we have seen, is not as efficient as a monetary trading system.

Its no good paying German exporters in United States dollars, because German exporters have to pay German manufacturers in the same currency that they pay to their employees, and German employees want to be paid in Deutschmarks not dollars, if only for the sensible reason that there is not a lot they can buy from German shops with another country's currency.

Hence, exporters want to be paid in their own currency, while importers prefer to pay in their own currency (after all the importers operate in a monetary system that uses their own currency). Some mechanism has to be available that enables both exporters and importers to use the currencies of their choice.

That mechanism is the system of international currency exchange. There is a world market for each country's currency, and, like any other market, it operates on the basis of demand and supply, though, unlike most other markets, it can be subject to significant intervention by governments attempting to forestall the effects of demand and supply.

If someone in Ogoland wants to import fleets of German Mercedes cars for sale to fellow Ogolanders, he must, somewhere along the line, acquire sufficient German Deutschmarks to meet the purchase price of the cars from the German exporter. Naturally, when it comes to selling Mercedes cars in Ogoland they will be sold for Ogoland currency, i.e. quonks, for Ogolanders do not have any other currency at their disposal.

Likewise, if a German importer of cocoa (the prime ingredient in the world famous German chocolate) wants to purchase twenty thousand tons of prime Ogoland cocoa ('Kwagasane Number 1'), he will have to acquire quonks to make the purchase. Having purchased the cocoa for quonks, he will, however, sell it on to German chocolate manufacturers for German Deutschmarks, there not being many Germans about with spare stocks of Ogoland quonks!

Fortunately, there is a foreign exchange rate between German Deutschmarks and Ogoland quonks, as there is between Deutschmarks and all currencies that are traded. Last time I looked at the exchange rates, 10 Deutschmarks would buy 100 quonks (they would also buy £2.50 in British pounds sterling, which means that 100 quonks would buy £2.50 British pounds). Hence, the Ogoland importer would simply look up the Deutschmark – quonk exchange rate (1:10), note the Deutschmark price that the German exporter is quoting for a Mercedes in Germany, (say, 25,000 DM), and he would know how many quonks he would require from his bank to buy the Deutschmarks to pay the importer for each Mercedes he imports (Q250,000).

If, of course, the Mercedes are shipped in a Swedish roll-on roll-off ship, the importer will have to buy Swedish kroner with his quonks, and he would need to look-up the kroner-quonk exchange rate to know how much it will cost him (and he will need to buy British pounds to pay his insurance premium at Lloyd's in case the ship is lost with his cargo in it).

It does not matter whether the importer changes quonks into Deutschmarks (or any other currency), or the exporter takes quonks and changes them himself. Ultimately, the exchange will have to be made by one or other person in the chain, and when the change is made it can make a difference to the final price paid in the exporter's currency, for exchange rates can be volatile – up one day and down the next.

If you hold quonks when they are falling in price in terms of other currencies, you could suffer a loss because when you come to sell them you will get fewer dollars, Deutschmarks, pounds, yen, francs, kroner, rupees or whatever, than you would have got if you had sold them earlier. If, on the other hand, you hold on to your quonks when they are rising in price in terms of foreign currencies, you could make an extra profit, because when you come to sell them you will get more dollars, etc., per quonk than you would have done if you had sold them earlier.

The possibility of gains and losses in buying and selling foreign currency, makes for an international market in the currencies themselves. Banks, speculators and institutions specialise in trading in foreign currency, holding on to one country's money, while selling off another's. They study the market, watching for signs of any prospective change in demand or supply of particular currencies and make ready to move into or out of currencies to make profits and avoid losses.

Currency rates can change rapidly, perhaps because of the policies being pursued by a government, or because a government is not managing its problems all that well, or because of the underlying economic trends in certain commodities (oil, cocoa, rubber, coffee, tin, etc.), or because of threats and rumours of war, unrest, drought and disease, or whatever. Sometimes the reasons are real – there is something actually happening that deserves to result in a change in a country's exchange rate – and sometimes the reasons are imaginary, in the minds of the speculators. Here the market reacts to its prejudices and beliefs about what is to happen rather than to concrete evidence that it will – perhaps the coming to power of a certain political ruler will panic the markets when they should be pacified, or pacify them when they should panic.

You should by now be getting a flavour of the potential instability in world currency markets, and be wondering what can be done to avoid wild fluctuations in exchange rates, given the harmful effects such fluctuations can have on international trade. That these effects can be harmful does not require much imagination to appreciate. If you are an exporter, and your country's currency is wildly fluctuating, or you believe it is likely to fluctuate during the time between when you ship your goods and receive your payment, you are more likely to be inhibited from entering into export contracts than if you are fairly sure that the price you agree to sell them at in June will be realised when you cash the importer's bank drafts in August.

The perception of the individual exporter (or importer) is only a part of the picture. The aggregate actions of all exporters and importers in a country have an effect on the value of the currency, and this value is normally of considerable concern to the government. The rate of exchange of a currency in terms of other currencies is partly a consequence of the independent decisions of thousands of exporters and importers. As they sell and buy goods, they require either to sell foreign currency to convert their export earnings into their own currency, or to buy foreign currency to convert their own currency into foreign currencies. The aggregate of their actions will determine how much foreign currency is needed to carry out international trade.

If exporters earn more than importers purchase, the country will have a net surplus of foreign currency at its disposal, suggesting a strong domestic currency in international markets (more foreigners require your country's banknotes than your people require foreign banknotes).

If importers purchase more than exporters sell, the country will have a net deficit of foreign currency, suggesting a weakening domestic currency in international markets (more of your citizens require foreign banknotes than foreigners require your banknotes).

Having looked at one side of the consequences of international trade, and noted that, as a result of the actions of individuals in your own and other countries, the exchange rates of all trading currencies for each other will fluctuate, sometimes wildly, according to demand and supply (some currencies, you should note are not used in trade because the governments concerned do not wish them to be, or because traders do not believe these currencies are worth trading in at all), we will now turn to look at the effects of the balance of payments on the internal economy, and the effects of the internal economy on the balance of payments.

We begin with a short salute to another of Scotland's early philosopher-economists, David Hume, a contemporary and good friend of Adam Smith at Edinburgh University. His name is associated with the *gold specie* approach to the balance of payments, in which he attacked the then prevailing idiocy in public policy which asserted, among other things, that a country grew rich by piling up surpluses of gold and by following anti-trade policies that prevented gold leaving the country.

With an international gold standard, trade took place with each country's currency fixed in terms of every other country's currency. Given the efficient working of the quantity theory of money ($MV = PT$), an inflow would be increased when your exports were paid for by the importing countries in gold bullion, provided that you received more for exports than you paid in imports, which would increase the money supply of your country.

This would raise domestic prices in the country with the gold surplus, and reduce them in the country(ies) with a gold deficit. The effect would be to make your domestic prices higher than foreign prices, and this would encourage imports to your country of goods to compete with your domestic output. Exports would contract (faced with lower domestic prices abroad) and imports expand (faced with higher domestic prices at home). The result: gold would flow out of the country and your price level would fall back towards competitive prices compared with foreign prices.

Hume regarded the gold standard as an automatic adjustment mechanism. Governments that followed policies of deliberately acquiring gold surpluses from trade, perhaps by subsidising exports or offering monopolies to domestic traders, while restricting imports, perhaps by forcing all goods for trade to be sent or delivered in ships owned by its own nationals, and prohibiting the export of technology, or even of the people who understood the technology, were ensuring that a nation would be poorer than it needed to be.

Having prevented the automatic adjustment mechanism from operating, the government was also forcing up domestic prices without the compensating process of lower-priced imports becoming available. The countries, formerly willing and able, because they had gold stocks, to import the restricting countries' exports, are now less able, even if as willing, to purchase them. Not only have the export prices risen but also the countries wishing to import the goods have less gold available to pay for them. International trade would, in these circumstances, be curbed, and with it the rising living standards brought about by international trade.

Hume, of course, was absolutely right, and his view eventually triumphed over the prevailing views of the gold hoarders. It is, however, sad to note, that though the world monetary system has changed a great deal since Hume's day, and that we no longer have a gold standard with its automatic mechanism for adjustment, many of the restrictive trade practices of the previous era (mandatory use of a national shipping line, subsidies to exports, curbs on imports, etc.) have reasserted themselves in international trade and they have the same effect of curbing international trade to the detriment of the living standards of all countries.

In the modern world economy, there are two main systems of foreign exchange management: the fixed or floating systems.

Under a regime of fixed exchange rates, only the government can alter the price of a currency in terms of other currencies; it announces the rate of exchange of quonks for Deutschmarks and all other trading currencies and determines to maintain that rate of exchange whatever happens to the trade balance.

If foreigners sell quonks to obtain foreign currency, the government orders the central bank to buy as many quonks from foreigners as are offered at the official exchange rate; if foreigners buy quonks with foreign currency, the Bank sells as many quonks as are demanded at the official exchange rate. By the sheer authority of the Bank, and its ability to fund sales or purchases at the official rate, the government hopes that it can maintain the official rate throughout temporary crises of surplus or deficit demands for its currency.

Inevitably, if the underlying trading relations (a large and sustained balance of payments deficit or surplus) suggest that a currency is over- or under-priced in terms of other currencies, there will come a time when the Bank will have to inform the government that it does not have sufficient reserves of foreign currency to keep buying the national currency, or that its accumulation of foreign reserves is so high that the current fixed price of domestic currency is too low.

The government must then decide whether, or rather when, to adjust the fixed price of the domestic currency. It must do this by *devaluation* if foreign exchange reserves (including gold) are too low, or by *revaluation* if foreign exchange reserves are too high. Governments that operate fixed exchange rates tend, however, to be very firmly convinced that the rate they have chosen (or inherited from a previous government) is the right rate, and they, therefore, often delay adjusting the fixed rate, sometimes beyond the point where it is clearly necessary. This leads to devaluations or revaluations that are insufficiently convincing to the international money markets, and speculation that a further adjustment will soon be necessary continues.

If these discrepancies between the official rate and the 'true' rate persist for long enough, informal black markets are likely to appear. Visitors to these countries can be beseiged by locals offering them extravagantly better rates of exchange for their foreign currency in local currency (a common enough experience in Soviet and Eastern European countries and in certain Third World countries). Eventually, of course, the government must bow to economic realities and adjust its exchange rates.

A flexible exchange rate does not require discretionary actions by the Bank or the government, because the foreign exchange rate adjusts itself in the light of trading conditions.

If exporters are cashing foreign currency earnings in excess of the amounts that importers are buying foreign currency to pay for their imports, there will be a tendency for the price of the domestic currency to rise because the supply of foreign currency from exporters exceeds the demands for it from importers.

If the exporters are earning less foreign currency than importers require to pay for the country's imports, there will be a demand for foreign currency in excess of its supply and this will tend to reduce the price of the domestic currency and raise the price of foreign currency.

Meanwhile, in foreign countries, traders will be buying the domestic currency to pay for their imports (your exports) or selling it to convert their export earnings (your imports) into their own currencies. The net effect of this trading, plus the trading of speculators making judgements about the future movement of currency prices, and exporters and importers expecting to require certain amounts of currencies in the future when they settle their accounts, will affect the selling price of each currency. Because the rate can float freely up or down, there is no problem for the government to attend to, and no problem with balance of payments surpluses or deficits.

Any tendency for a surplus to appear will raise the price of foreign currency relative to domestic currency (automatic revaluation, because our currency is too 'cheap'). Instead of, say, 10 quonks to the dollar, we will make it 5 quonks to the dollar, which means that an export costing 10 quonks at home and selling for a dollar abroad, will now cost 2 dollars abroad, but still only 10 quonks at home. This will reduce demand for our exports. We will get less foreign currency from our more expensive (in foreign currency) exports, thus reducing our export earnings.

It will also mean that we will have to pay out more foreign currency for the increased imports we buy, increasing import costs (what we buy for 10 quonks at home – but costing a dollar abroad – now costs us only 5 quonks at home – still a dollar abroad – and we would expect our demand for imports to grow at this lower domestic price). This will bring export earnings into balance with import costs and eliminate the surplus that was appearing at the old prices.

The exact converse will occur if a deficit appears in the accounts; foreign currency will become cheaper (automatic devaluation, because our currency is too 'dear') relative to our currency. We will get more foreign currency from our exports, and we will pay out less foreign currency for the imports we buy. Instead of 10 quonks to the dollar, we make it, say, 20 quonks to the dollar, which means that an export costing 10 quonks at home and selling for a dollar abroad will now sell for 50c abroad, which should increase foreign demand for our exports and boost our export earnings. An import, formerly costing 10 quonks to buy at home, though costing a dollar abroad, will now cost 20 quonks at home and still a dollar abroad, which should reduce our imports and our import costs.

Naturally, these arithmetical examples exaggerate the rise and fall of foreign currency prices in a flexible system. It is more likely that the adjustments would be quite small – a few fractions of a cent at a time, though these fractions can cumulate quickly in certain circumstances and provide a major shift in exchange rates. But in a freely floating exchange rate system, the adjustment, being automatic, will be immediate and there will be no change in the foreign currency reserves.

In fact, with a pure floating rate there is no real need for reserves at all, for the entire burden of adjustment falls on the sellers of exports and the buyers of imports, who respond to price changes by adjusting the amounts of goods that they buy and sell. Reserves are required only if the adjustment processes in the real economy are too slow (or too disruptive) to take effect and the country must defend its currency's parities immediately.

Of course, in the real world, some combination of reserves and dependence on economic adjustments between exporters and importers is required. This is sometimes given the inelegant, though expressive title, of a 'dirty' floating currency. It is what happens when a government permits its currency to 'float' but only gently, intervening with its currency reserves if the rise or decline in its currency's parities with foreign currencies threatens international confidence in its economic stability.

Chapter 29

Balance of payments

WHATEVER SYSTEM OF FOREIGN EXCHANGE ACCOUNTS a country operates, be it based on an immutable (or almost immutable) fixed rate or be it freely flotating or a managed float (sometimes called a 'dirty' float), it will still need to prepare its balance of payments accounts as part of its national statistics. These accounts outline the trading position of a country, and also the extent to which it has received capital flows from other countries.

The United Nations Organisation has contributed a great deal to the production of standardised accounts by its member states. This enables comparisons to be made between states on their trading performances. Rather than develop a set of standard UN accounts here, I have decided to present the accounts in a way that brings out the main economic points about them. You can supplement this chapter with a scrutiny of your own country's accounts, making sure when you do that you carefully read the small print and footnotes that accompany them.

Broadly, the payments accounts should include data under two major headings: the *current* account and the *capital* account. These correspond to the economic activities of the country in the conduct of its relationships with other countries.

Taking the current account first, we can note that this normally is a good indicator of the net trading position of a country's goods and services. The 'trade balance' refers to items in this account. The *visibles* (so-called because the customs officials can actually see them physically) are real goods that cross the frontier in both directions. The *invisibles* consist of earnings or expenditures on services of one kind or another.

Visible exports consist of food and raw materials, finished (i.e. ready for immediate consumption) and semi-finished (i.e. requiring some additional processing) manufactured goods, and other tangible goods.

All countries import food, sometimes out of absolute necessity because domestic production cannot cover home consumption (deliberately in the case, say, of the United Kingdom, which abandoned self-sufficiency in food in favour of concentrating on manufacturing, and by the failure of domestic agricultural policies in the case of the Soviet Union), or because the country prefers certain delicacies from abroad that it cannot produce for climatic or other reasons. Hence, though the United States is a producer of grain for the world, it also imports food from abroad (mangoes from the Caribbean, Scottish salmon, Polish smoked meats, German sausage, Italian olives, etc.).

Some countries have virtually no raw materials within them and they have to import almost everything that they need, including oil. Britain has substantial coal reserves, which will last for a couple of hundred years, and substantial oil resources in the North Sea (which will last at least until about 2020). Almost every other raw material is imported. The United States, which has vast supplies of many raw materials, is a major importer of those materials that it does not have, or finds too expensive at current world prices to procure domestically.

Industrialised countries export and import manufactured and semi-manufactured goods. The components for computers and word processors, for example, may be manufactured in many countries and assembled in Europe or North America. If you look in the back of your computer you will see parts with labels from places as far apart as Taiwan, Germany, Scotland, USA, Korea and Japan.

A country's invisible trade can be a major item in its foreign earnings. Britain's invisible exports are equal to more than half the earnings from its visibles, reflecting its position as a major financial centre in the world (banking, finance, insurance, brokerage, legal services, etc.), and, also, a major supplier of shipping and aircraft services. In addition, earnings from royalties (books, videos, films, patents, etc.), consultancy fees, marketing, including advertising, and management contracts, plus remitted profits and dividends from ownership of overseas companies, amount to a major proportion of the invisibles.

Government contributions to international bodies (the United Nations, for example), military and development aid, and grants to other countries, must be netted with flows, if any, in the opposite direction. Some countries receive substantial aid in one form or another, and in so far as this is in the form of money it will appear as invisible transfers.

Private individuals also engage in net transfers abroad. Many residents from abroad working in a country remit part of their earnings to their families back home. In the Middle East, large numbers of Palestinians work in many Arab countries, as do Pakistanis, Koreans and British. Their remittances back home are an invisible debit on their host country's balance of payments, and an invisible credit as far as their own countries are concerned.

The method of calculating the trade balance is to net export earnings from all sources against import expenditures. It may be that the visible trade is in deficit (more imports than exports) but that the invisible trade is in surplus (more exports than imports), or vice versa. If they are both in deficit over a long period, this suggests that the country is not managing its trading affairs as well as it might. Corrective action, of one kind or another, will eventually be necessary, and, indeed, it might very well be a condition of receiving international aid (from such organisations as the International Monetary Fund) that a country put into effect specific policies aimed at tackling whatever fundamental problems are causing its imbalance.

Alternatively, if a country has a steady source of funds that make up the trade imbalance (as Cuba has from the Soviet Union and Israel has from the United States) it can continue with its domestic policies and ignore any structural requirements to alter its policies that might be suggested by international agencies, or indeed, economists who have been asked (hopefully for a fee!) to advise it.

The capital account in the balance of payments accounts is separated conceptually from the current balance as it records the flows of, mainly, investment funds into and out of the country. By investment flows we do not mean the physical investment in plant and machinery, which has been our meaning so far. This little confusion is typical of the way economists and accountants do not always see eye to eye in the matter of definitions!

An investment flow in the balance of payments accounts is a financial flow from one country to another, the purpose of which might very well be to purchase a plant for physical production. The accounts measure the financial flow as a capital transaction. If the wholly owned plant abroad purchases machine tools from the country whose residents own it, this will appear in the current account as an export from the owning country, but the transfer of the funds to the plant is, in the first place, an outflow of capital. The return flow of profits and dividends will, as stated above, appear as an invisible credit on the current account.

A major company – an oil major, a multinational computer company, a major car manufacturer, etc. – may decide to borrow money in one country (because the terms are more attractive than loans offered by other countries), and apply those funds to expand a plant in a second country. The capital account will show those funds flowing from the lender country to the country where they are to be applied.

In contrast, a wealthy Kuwaiti businessman may decide to purchase shares in a European company, or to acquire government bonds issued by a foreign state. The flow of funds for this type of portfolio acquisition will appear as a credit in the receiving country's capital account. If you like, you can consider the sending of the share certificate or the government bond as an export, albeit of paper, which is a credit to the balance of payments account.

Naturally, countries which have a flow of investment funds (direct and portfolio) leaving the country, as companies invest in their overseas subsidiaries and individuals acquire shares or bonds from abroad, might also have a flow in the reverse direction, with overseas companies and individuals engaging in direct or portfolio investment in the domestic territory. The net overseas investment flow will, if positive, either add to the surplus on the trade balance, or reduce the deficit if there is one. If the flow is negative, it will reduce the surplus or increase the deficit.

Other items in the capital accounts cover the flows of funds that cover for potential defaults by foreign traders (being liquidated as exporters' invoices are paid); foreign currency lending by domestic and foreign banks; and changes in the holdings of the domestic currency by foreign banks. Again these flows are netted to produce a positive or negative entry in the balance of payments. A balance of payments account could look something like Table 6.

The balance of payments accounts will always balance because they are a form of double entry book-keeping. If there is a trade deficit this does

TABLE 6: **Balance of paments accounts**

Current account		
Visibles		
Exports		
Imports		
Visible trade balance:	+	−
Invisibles		
Credits		
Debits		
Invisible balance:	+	−
Current account balance:	+	−
Capital account		
Investment in foreign countries		
Direct		
Portfolio		
Foreign inward investment		
Direct		
Portfolio		
Private investment balance:	+	−
Government capital investment:	+	−
Trade credit		
Import credit received		
Export credit given		
Net credit received:	+	−
Other capital transactions		
Net foreign currency lending abroad		
Changes in own currency liabilities		
External lending by own banks		
Other		
Total:	+	−
Capital account balance:	+	−
Overall balance:	+	−

not mean that foreigners are awaiting payment. All deficits must be funded in some way, perhaps by running down reserves, perhaps by an international loan. The balance of payments accounts will show how the trade imbalance is being funded.

A deficit that persists will sooner or later run out of the means by which it can be funded, and long before this unhappy situation arises traders will become wary of entering into contracts with the country concerned (the balance of payments accounts are public documents, and traders, or their bankers, can scrutinise them, and with a free press details of potential defaulters will be publicised widely across the world).

If the country is operating a fixed exchange regime it will be under heavy pressure to devalue the exchange rate. If it is managing a floating exchange regime it will be under pressure to ease off its controls and let the currency devalue gradually. If it is pursuing domestic expansionary policies that are sucking in imports without raising domestic output it will be under heavy pressure to curb these credit policies and take stiffer austerity measures to reduce imports. If it is funding its deficit by borrowing from international banks, or the IMF, it will be urged to tackle its domestic problems on the one hand, and find itself being avoided by international lenders on the other.

In short, a persistent deficit would eventually have to be tackled by one or other (unpopular) policy. The policies would be unpopular because everybody likes to enjoy a higher standard of living than circumstances justify, as long as somebody else is paying for it.

In the case of a country with a persistent surplus, the policy responses may be symmetrically opposite to those of a deficit country, but the economic leverage on such a country is nowhere nearly as powerful. Surplus countries can ignore pleas to revalue because they do not have creditors on their doorsteps. By failing to revalue they are acting like those countries who hoarded gold and silver in the eighteenth century, and who were criticised for so doing by David Hume.

A country in persistent surplus is in effect exporting real goods and services to importers and being paid in foreign currency (paper) for them. It could be argued that if a surplus country prefers to accumulate paper money in exchange for real goods and services, it is acting somewhat irrationally. If it spent the foreign currency (on imports from the deficit economies) it would be exchanging paper for real goods. By holding on to paper currency it is foregoing real goods for paper.

But this is the problem. Its preference for paper is 'good' on one level but 'bad' on the other. It drains off money into its bank vaults which acts as a withdrawal from the circular flow of income of the importing country. By not spending its export earnings it reduces economic activity in importing countries, and, in the long run, helps to keep the world economy operating at a lower level of activity.

Compelling a surplus country to re-cycle its foreign earnings is no easy task. International pressure can do only so much, but, in the end, the importing countries could be driven to the extreme of retaliating with import restrictions. This, however, would be a definite blow at consumer living standards in the importing country – residents are buying the foreign goods presumably because they prefer them to domestic goods. It would also not necessarily achieve the desired result of expanding world trade, particularly if it sparked off a trade war and a break-down in the international trading system. Gentle, persistent, and firm persuasion is probably the only hope, whereas with deficit countries a firm refusal to fund their deficits will soon bring them to the negotiating table, though even here it is necessary to tread carefully, because one country's deficit is another country's surplus, and a sudden collapse in any country's economy brought about by pre-emptory action could be a damaging blow to international trade (and credit).

Chapter 30

Concluding remarks

I HOPE THAT BY THIS STAGE IN YOUR READING of the book you have got more than an appetite for continuing your studies of macroeconomics. We have covered a great deal of ground, much of it by only skimming the surface of certain topics, other parts by stripping out all the complications that influence macroeconomic decisions in the real world. But, I hope that what you have been exposed to has caused you to think, perhaps for the first time, about the very real and important policy issues that all governments, in all countries, have to grapple with as best as they can.

Macroeconomics is not a settled body of doctrine. It remains a subject of continuing controversy, at the very heart of the democratic process. In the industrialised world, macroeconomics is about managing highly complex and extremely wealthy countries; in the Third World, it faces no lesser challenges as governments battle with the problems of slow, though persistent, economic growth and the much faster growing aspirations and continuing real needs of millions of people.

In order to help you consider how best to continue your studies of macroeconomics, I thought it might be useful to suggest one or two books that you should find readable and rewarding. Of course, this does not preclude you from browsing in your local bookshop or in the library. My suggestions are aimed at taking your studies a stage or more further, and you will find the books mentioned rather more difficult than this text. I have refrained, however, from suggesting titles that are best reserved for formally taught courses, both to save you feeling that you have been dropped in at the deep end, and also, because your teachers will want to make their own suggestions for course textbooks.

In Part I we looked at national income accounting, and, without doubt, the most readable survey of national income accounts is Wilfred Beckerman's *Introduction to National Income Analysis* (Allen & Unwin, London), first published in 1968, and since on sale in a 2nd edition. You might also care to note that Beckerman wrote a masterly survey of the arguments among economists on the subject of economic growth: *In Defence of Economic Growth* (Cape, London), 1974.

Keynesian economics dominate the textbooks and you should have no trouble at all in finding much to read about Keynes, his writing, his policies, and what has come to be known as 'Keynesian' economics.

A fine introduction to many of the issues is Michael Stewart's, *Keynes and After* (3rd Edition, Penguin Books, Harmondsworth, 1986), which can be read in conjunction with *Inflation: a guide to the crisis in economics* (Penguin Books, Harmondsworth, 1977 by J. A. Trevithick. These should give you a good grounding in Keynesian and monetarist economics, and most of the topics discussed in Parts II and III.

A more advanced survey of monetarist economics will be found in *Monetarism: theory, evidence & policy*, by Howard Vane and John Tompson (Martin Robertson, Oxford, 1980). If you can stand the slightly stiffer pace there is an excellent text by K. A. Chrystal: *Controversies in British Macroeconomics*, (2nd Edition, Philip Allan, London, 1983), which uses the actual econometric models (or, rather very simplified versions of them) to elucidate the main issues that separate a Keynesian from a monetarist position.

Professor G. K. Shaw has produced yet another well written and crystal clear text in his latest: *Rational Expectations: an elementary exposition*, (Harvester Press, Brighton, 1984), and, given the importance of the theories of rational expectations in current controversies, an acquaintance with this topic is essential.

For topics that are covered in Part IV, I suggest that you consult any elementary economics textbook. International trade, at least in the mechanisms of trade relations, if not in the policy conclusions, is at present not all that controversial compared with the issues raised by monetarism and rational expectations (what a dangerous statement that is in macroeconomics!). This is reflected in the current dearth of primer texts in trade theory and the balance of payments. All I can say is that while debate continues between protectionists and free-traders, it tends to be confined to the ranks of lobbyists for producers and the government. As far as economists are concerned the subject is 'very quiet' or is now settled.

As you get into your studies in economics, you will find that there is a tendency in many texts to use what look like complicated mathematics and statistics in many of the presentations of the various debates. This can be off-putting for those whose mathematics are 'rusty', but it ought not to be a permanent barrier to your interest in and enjoyment of the study of economics.

Might I suggest, somewhat immodestly, but on a principle akin to the right of a cook to test his own food – which is why there are very few thin cooks! – that if you find mathematics or statistics a little daunting you consult a couple of my own books? If you are interested in a gentle approach to quantitative methods, dip into: *Mathematics for Innumerate Economists* (Duckworth, London, 1982) and *Invitation to Statistics* (Blackwell, Oxford, 1983).

I have reserved almost to the last any mention of the other side of a macroeconomic approach to the economy, namely that of a microeconomic approach. Just as macroeconomics is based on the aggregate view, microeconomics is based on the individual view, as seen by the

Concluding remarks · 165

consumer or the business manager. No study of economics is complete without a thorough grounding in both approaches.

A companion volume in this series called *Microeconomics*, (mentioned earlier in this book) has been written by Ronald Shone of Stirling University. It should be consulted by all serious students.

Lastly, might I offer a final piece of advice when studying economics (which like all advice is not mandatory!). That economics is controversial ought not to be news to you by now. That it can be extremely interesting, ought also to be familiar to you, though, perhaps, the evidence of this text may not be sufficient to sustain such an assertion!

But a knowledge of economics is not a panacea for the world's problems – it so often can be the beginning of a problem in itself. Good commonsense is required when advising people, governments or the world, on which economic policy they ought to be following to solve this or that crisis.

If economists, and those who claim to act on their prescriptions, were to show the same humility that they expect, and require, from those listening to them, and if they were to approach their certainties with a trifle more uncertainty that they have got it right (this time!), then perhaps the world might be a little closer to solving its problems, and a little more peaceful in the way it goes about its business.

After all, economists are only human, and, therefore, are by definition, far from perfect and we have still a lot to learn.

Index

absolute advantage, 142–5, 147
aggregate demand, 88, 92, 122
aid, 19
animal spirits, 82, 115
arbitrage, 96, 137
Australian penal colony, 99
autarky, 138

balanced budget, 89, 90
balance of payments, 152–3, 158–62
  capital account, 157, 159
  current account, 157, 159
banks, 82, 104, 107, 111, 151, 154, 160
  notes, 101, 105, 107, 152
  multiplier, 109–10
barter, 93, 94, 102, 150
boom, 90–91
bonds, 112–13, 115, 159
borrowing, 38, 81, 83, 84, 109–10, 112
budget deficit, 90
built in stabiliser, 90–91
Burns, Robert, 67
businesses, 21–22, 26–28, 30, 33, 46, 49, 55, 63, 67, 68, 70, 73, 77, 81, 82, 85, 102, 112, 114, 116–118, 121–2, 125, 128, 130

capital, 38, 49, 56, 63, 69, 77, 82, 84, 139, 141
  circulating, 63–4, 73
  fixed, 63–4, 147
capitalism, 24, 27–9, 60, 73, 82, 120, 138–9
Captain Cook, 97
cash, 83
central bank, 111–14, 119
census, 18
cheque, 107–8, 110–11, 113, 116

circular flow, 22–3, 50, 67
  government, 24–9
  trade, 30–34
classical economists, 61, 66, 116–19, 120–22, 135
communism, 128, 130
comparative advantage, 143–9
consumption, 18, 21–2, 36–37, 40, 50, 55, 62, 70, 71, 72, 73, 75, 76, 78, 87
  function, 61, 72, 73, 78
cost push, 89
costs, 39, 41, 44, 46, 48, 52, 56, 121, 126, 142
credit, 106
currency, 57, 107, 116, 150, 154–55
current account, 107–8

Davenant, Charles, 17
defence, 12, 13, 38, 54–5, 88, 128, 140
deficient demand, 88
deflationary gap, 88
demand management, 88–9, 91–2, 123, 129
deposit accounts, 108–10
depreciation, 41, 49, 55
depression, 88, 90
derived demand, 69, 77, 79, 120
disposable income, 90
division of labour 138
devaluation, 154, 161

econometrics, 124, 164
education, 13
effective demand, 67, 69, 71, 79, 87, 125
employment, 45, 47, 49, 62, 64, 67, 86, 120, 136, 148
equilibrium, 33, 67, 69, 71, 75, 76, 78, 120, 126, 133

European Economic Community, 141
exchange, 40, 84, 93, 138
expectations, 81, 82, 85, 90, 126, 130, 133, 135
expenditure, 16, 36, 50, 54
exports, 18, 31–4, 39, 129, 139, 145, 150–5, 157

factors of production, 23, 67
fiscal drag, 131, 135
fiscal policies, 87, 91, 128, 131, 136
foreign exchange, 58, 150–56, 157, 161
foreign trade, see international trade
flexible exchange rate, 154, 156
fractional reserve, 109
free trade, 146, 149
frictional unemployment, 64, 66, 88, 123–5
Friedman, Milton, 123–4, 127, 130, 132
full employment, 76, 80, 82, 85, 87, 88, 119, 120–23, 128, 130

gold, 104–6, 153
government, 24–9, 32–4, 38–9, 46, 57, 58, 62, 64, 69, 80, 82, 84–5, 87, 88, 91, 98, 101, 102, 107, 110, 111, 119, 122, 125, 128, 129, 130, 131, 133, 134, 135, 143, 148, 150–1, 154, 163
gross domestic product, 45, 48
gross investment, 37
gross national income, see national income
gross national product (GNP), 35, 38, 44, 89, 144
  measures, 44–50, 59
  real, 58
growth, 12, 38, 43, 44, 54, 56, 60, 102, 130, 141, 147, 163

haggle, 94, 96–97
households, 21–2, 24–8, 30, 33, 35, 40, 43, 48–50, 57, 62, 67, 68, 70, 71, 72, 74, 77, 81, 87, 88, 89, 90, 102, 112, 116, 117–19, 120–22, 125, 126, 130

Hume, David, 153, 161
hyper-inflation, 124, 129

imports, 18, 31–4, 39, 79, 139–41, 143, 145, 150–55, 157
income, 16, 50, 62, 72, 78, 90, 117, 131,
  distribution, 19
inflation, 43, 56, 57, 61, 88, 89, 92, 101, 102, 119, 123–4, 126–8, 129, 130, 131, 133, 134, 135, 136, 164
injection, 71, 77, 79, 128, 130
inputs, 22, 26, 37, 67
international trade, 7, 30, 39, 48, 138–142, 150–3
interest, 22, 28, 70, 81, 83, 84, 85, 108–9, 111, 113–15
intervention, 135
investment, 29, 37, 40, 48, 49, 70, 71, 72, 74, 76–78, 81, 82, 84, 109–10, 122–3, 126, 133
invisibles, 157–8

job search, 124–5, 130

Keynes, John Maynard, 60–61, 66, 69, 71, 72, 73, 75, 78, 80, 82, 83, 84, 85, 104, 115, 117, 122, 129, 135
Keynsian economics, 60–61, 79–80, 84, 85, 87, 91, 123, 126, 128, 130, 131–2, 133–4, 163
King, Gregory, 17–18

labour, 22, 26, 37, 43, 46, 50, 57, 66, 67, 68, 69, 71, 77, 117, 120–22, 123, 124, 126, 137
leisure, 54
lender of last resort, 111
liquidity preference, 84, 85
living standards, 93–4, 138, 162
loans, 22

market economy, 130, 135
  sector, 44–6, 62
marginal productivity, 121
marginal propensity to
  consume, 61, 72, 78–9
  save, 61, 72, 78–9, 87

measurable economic welfare
  (MEW), 54–5
merit goods, 89
models, 20–34, 71, 72, 88, 122, 133
monetarism, 61, 92, 117, 128–32, 164
money, 14, 52–3, 57, 74, 81, 83, 93, 96, 97, 99–101, 106, 118, 128, 154
  balances, 117
  creation of, 108–12
  demand, 116–19
  instructions, 82
  role of, 102
  supply, 84, 111, 114–15, 119, 130, 134, 135, 153
multiplier, 61, 78–9, 84, 85, 86, 109–10, 122
morals, 12

national income/(expenditure), 14, 16–19, 35–9, 43, 52, 59, 80, 91, 118, 163
natural unemployment, 121–7, 129–30, 134, 136
negotiate, 39–40, 84, 126, 133, 162
net investment, 37, 56
net national income, 49
net national product, 56
net property income, 45
non-market sector, 44, 57, 62
Nordhaus, William, 54

'Ogoland', 44, 108–10, 116, 150–1
open market operations (OMO), 111–15
opportunity cost, 55, 144–5
output, 18, 21–22, 25, 31, 37, 41–2, 46, 49–50, 65, 69, 71, 72, 77, 87, 88, 120, 122, 125, 130, 135, 136

Phillips Curve, 123–5, 127, 133–4
planning, 82, 91
Petty, William, 16, 18
Pigou, A.C., 52, 57
pollution, 53, 54, 57
poverty, 26, 54, 65
price, 41–3, 58, 66, 68, 87, 96, 118–19, 120–22, 126, 133, 134–5, 137, 153, 156

production, 21
productive labour, 44
productivity, 133–4, 138, 146
profit, 28, 41, 42–3, 44, 45, 47, 48, 55, 73, 181–2, 105, 110, 114, 151
protection, 143, 146, 147–8, 164
public expenditure, 13, 38–9, 90, 128
public works, 85–6
precautionary motive, 83
purchasing power, 102, 116, 121–2

quantity theory of money, 116–19, 133, 135, 153

rational expectations, 133–7, 164
real wages, 121–2, 124–6, 134
rents, 22, 28, 36, 45, 47, 57
reserve rates, 112–13
reserves, 156
residual, 50
repatriated profits, 48–9
revaluation, 154, 161
Ricardo, David, 144
risk, 81, 135

sales revenue, 42, 45–6, 125
satisfaction, 35–6
saving, 16, 26, 34, 49, 61, 62, 70, 71, 72, 74, 76, 109–10
Say, J.B., 68
securities, 82, 113
services, 23, 26–7, 83, 93
self sufficiency, 93, 140–1
Smith, Adam, 11, 12, 13, 30, 36, 44–5, 60, 139, 141, 153
social security, 26, 91
social wage, 89
socialism, 24, 27, 82, 128, 138–9
special deposits, 112
specialisation, 138
speculative motive, 83
stagflation, 127–8
stagnation, 11–12, 54, 127
statistics, 18, 19, 36, 40, 47, 49, 50, 51, 54, 56, 58, 62, 157
structural unemployment, 65, 88
subsidies, 24, 28, 136

tariffs, 150
taxation, 7, 16, 25–6, 33, 38, 55, 62, 79, 82, 87, 88, 89, 90, 92, 112, 131, 141
technology, 77, 140–41, 148, 153
Tobin, James, 54
trade, see exchange
trade union, 65, 66, 89, 122, 131, 133, 149
transfer payments, 26, 32, 65
transaction costs, 94, 95
transaction motives, 83, 97, 107, 116–17, 119

unemployment, 18, 26, 29, 61, 62, 64, 65, 69, 71, 72, 76, 86, 87, 90, 91, 120, 122–4, 126, 129, 130–1, 133

value added, 40–44, 45, 46, 49, 53
value judgements, 46, 52
velocity of circulation, 117–18
visibles, 157–8

wages, 22, 28, 33, 37, 41, 42–3, 44, 46, 61, 65, 69, 89, 120–22, 133, 135, 137, 148
wealth
  defined, 13–14
  creation, 25, 38, 104, 129
  measurement, 15, 116
welfare, 51–3, 128, 129

yield, 81, 82–3, 85, 114

The author of this Handbook

GAVIN KENNEDY was educated at the University of Strathclyde. He taught for two years at Brunel University, England and for eleven years at the Strathclyde Business School, Scotland. He is now Professor of Defence Finance at Heriot-Watt University, Edinburgh, Scotland.

His previous books include *The Military in the Third World* (1974), *The Economics of Defence* (1975), *The Death of Captain Cook* (1978), *Bligh* (1978), *Burden Sharing in NATO* (1979), *Mathematics for Innumerate Economists* (1982), *Defense Economics* (1983), and *Invitation to Statistics* (1984). He is the author of numerous articles on defence issues, and lectures widely in the UK, Australia and the USA on defence economics and procurement.